The Second
Most Important
Prayer

Romans 15:13

For the grace of God that brings salvation has appeared to all men. It teaches us to say "No" to ungodliness and worldly passions, and to live self-controlled, upright and godly lives in this present age, while we wait for the blessed hope—the glorious appearing of our great God and Savior, Jesus Christ, who gave himself for us to redeem us from all wickedness and to purify for himself a people that are his very own, eager to do what is good.

—Titus 2:11–14

If my people, who are called by my name, will humble themselves and pray and seek my face and turn from their wicked ways, then will I hear from heaven and will forgive their sin and will heal their land.

—2 Chronicles 7:14

Contents

Acknowledgments

To Denise—my wife and best friend, who has always stood with me, even when I'm not so likeable and lovable. God has blessed me more than I could ever have asked or imagined because of you.

To my children, Kristi and Bryan—watching you grow up has been such a joy. How completely blessed I am that God loaned you to me!

To my mom—thank you for always being there and supporting me and my family. You are the best mom ever!

To my brother, Bob—thank you for the sacrifices you made in your childhood because you needed to be the man of the family.

To Pastor Steve Struikmans—Thank you for your invaluable help with this book, and your anointed teaching over the years. What a spiritual inspiration you have been to me!

To Ernie Woolner—Thank you for your consistent encouragement, and the eternal investments you have and continue to make in me.

To Joe Alcorn—I am truly blessed to be your lifelong friend and brother in Christ.

To Sara Silfvast—Thank you for your friendship over the years and your help with this book. You are a cherished sister in Christ.

Abba, Father—I pray with all of my heart that this book honors and glorifies You. Thank You for everything You have done, are doing and will do for me. Thank You for never giving up on me. Thank You that Your faithfulness and love endure forever. You are the King of glory, the Lord Almighty. The One Who was, and is, and is to come. How completely awe-inspiring and magnificent You are! I love You with all of my heart. In Jesus' name. Amen.

Introduction

I AM A recovered backslidden Christian. I am a devoted disciple of Jesus Christ, who is learning to be a royal priest in God's holy kingdom (1 Peter 2:9). Though I asked Jesus Christ into my heart through *Young Life* at the age of sixteen or seventeen, I wasn't grounded in the Word, in fellowship, in discipleship, in church attendance, or in much of anything else godly. I really only wanted to fulfill my own desires. So I immediately and rapidly drifted.

I drifted for thirty years. And yet by virtually all worldly standards I was a success. I was a college graduate with an advanced degree. I was a U.S. Naval aviator. I'd completed two reserve commanding officer tours. I was a successful sales rep and manager with a major computer corporation and an internet software company. And I was a husband and father. I thought I had it all, that I could just worship God in my "own way." I was full of pride and I had a big ego.

Then my dad died.

That got me back to church (with my wife's urging). God began to speak very clearly to me, initially through my pastor's sermons. Finally, slowly, I began to listen.

I believe the most important decision we will ever make by far in life is to receive and believe in Jesus Christ. Romans 10:13 tells us, "Everyone who calls on the name of the Lord [Jesus Christ] will be saved."

I believe the second most important decision we will ever make is to surrender control of our lives to our Lord Jesus. Once you begin to experience the abundant life Jesus mentions in John 10:10, knowing God and making Him known on a journey toward Christ's likeness, you will never want to go back to your old ways. I know because I've lived on both sides. Only Jesus Christ can satisfy.

It has been almost nine years since I prayed what I believe is the second most important prayer we will ever pray—*"Lord Jesus, please take complete control of my life and make me the person You created me to be. Amen."* Making yourself available to God is a journey you don't want to miss! This journey is a blessing from God that is meant to be experienced, savored, and enjoyed, culminating with Jesus Christ Himself welcoming us into heaven.

Are you a new believer? Or has there been a time in your life when you were on fire for Jesus Christ but the flame died down? Perhaps you never grew closer to God. If this describes you, as it did me, this book will hopefully encourage you to dedicate every day you have left on this planet to Jesus Christ.

In it, I share my life experiences and lessons learned as a former backslidden (withering spiritually) Christian who started to listen when God called me to surrender my life to Him. Hopefully, you will be inspired to step out in faith to seek and fulfill the specific purpose that God has created you for (Ps. 138:8).

The Second Most Important Prayer contains practical tools on how be an active participant regarding your appointment as a royal priest in God's kingdom in order to "fight the good fight of the faith" (1 Tim. 6:12). It will take you through the journey of salvation and how God has set all believers apart for His sacred use. It will address how important it is that believers surrender their lives to Jesus Christ in order to faithfully represent God to a world that is literally dying to know Him. It includes practical tools on what to do now and valuable lessons learned along the way so that other travelers may be strengthened, encouraged, and comforted.

What you believe determines how you behave. Only a changed heart changes behavior. Only God can change the heart, but all Christians are called to be facilitators of change as ambassadors for Christ. Surrendering your life to Jesus Christ with a humble, contrite spirit will open your life to the abundant and rewarding spiritual life that will rock your world and the world around you.

Remember, it's not how you started; it's how you finish. Resolve in your heart to finish well so that God will be pleased and glorified by your life. Start today—it's a spectacular journey you don't want to miss!

The object of Christianity is not to sin less, but to glorify God more. It is not to somehow stop ourselves from doing the bad things we really want to do, but to find ourselves craving to do what pleases God.

—Charles F. Stanley

Heavenly and merciful Father, I have prayed that You will richly bless everyone who reads this book by revealing to them that the rich and abundant life You promise is available to anyone who will allow Jesus to take control of their lives; that if we humble ourselves under Your mighty hand, You will lift us up in due time. May our lives glorify You. In Jesus' name, Amen.

Chapter 1

The Most Important Prayer

WE ARE ALL sinful people whom a holy God invites, or *calls,* to come into a relationship with Him and be adopted into His family. However, we must come His way—through Jesus Christ—or we don't come at all.

> [If] you confess with your mouth, "Jesus is Lord," and believe in your heart that God raised him from the dead, you will be saved. For it is with your heart that you believe and are justified, and it is with your mouth that you confess and are saved… Everyone who calls on the name of the Lord will be saved.
>
> —Romans 10:9–10, 13

Salvation—Made New Because of God's Abounding Grace

We have all rebelled against God. We have all fallen short of the perfection required to enter into His heaven,[1] because we have all sinned by breaking at least one of God's Ten Commandments.

Some of the more obvious sins are lying, cheating, stealing, hating, lusting, dishonoring parents, using God's name in vain, coveting, envying, abusing, and committing adultery. Sin means *missing the mark*— God's standard of perfection. The punishment for sin is death.[2]

All of us are in a hopeless situation. None of us is perfect. We all have sinned (missed the mark of perfection). We continue to fall short of God's standard every day. How, then, can we get to heaven with the assurance of eternal life? God, of course, provides the answer.

Our lives need to be redeemed.

Redemption is delivery from bondage or slavery (in our case, to sin) by payment of a ransom. We all desperately need to be forgiven and restored into a right relationship with God. We need a Savior who offers us salvation that will completely redeem us from the penalty of our sins, someone who is qualified to pay our ransom.

God is so amazing. He chose to unconditionally love and redeem us, and even adopt us into His family, instead of banishing us for eternity! We are so incredibly blessed that Jesus Christ paid our ransom with His blood so we can go free.[3] He became the sin offering for us.[4]

Anyone can choose to be delivered from eternal death by receiving individual salvation through the payment of Christ's blood on the Cross because God, as an act of His will, chose to love us.[5] Our sin separated us from God, but Jesus Christ's sacrifice restored us to God. When we believe on and receive Jesus Christ in our hearts by faith, we become new creations.[6] We enter into a close personal relationship with the one true God who is our Father, our Savior (Jesus Christ), and our Teacher-Comforter-Counselor-Advocate (the Holy Spirit). That's why it's called the Good News!

Salvation is the glorification and exultation (elevation above all others) of God through the renewal of His creation. Humanity is reconciled (given restored fellowship, friendship, and peace) with God. Sin has completely corrupted the world, but God promises to make all things new.[7]

Salvation in Christ is best understood in three tenses: past, present, and future. When you believe in and receive Christ by faith, you are justified (God sees me "just [as] if I'd" never sinned)—saved from the punishment of sin. This is *past tense salvation,* a one-time event.

God has adopted you into His own family.[8] He sets you apart for His sacred use (sanctification) so you can grow spiritually into the likeness of Jesus Christ, so you can represent Him to an unbelieving world. You are saved from the power of sin.[9] This is *present tense salvation*; it remains ongoing all during your life on this planet.

Finally, *future tense salvation* is when we will be saved from the very presence of sin. It's called glorification.[10]

We will be in heaven, where there is no sin, with Jesus in the place He prepared in advance for us,[11] sharing in His glory. Incredible!

I don't know exactly what that means, but the apostle Paul summed it up when he wrote, "No eye has seen, no ear has heard, and no mind has imagined what God has prepared for those who love him" (1 Cor. 2:9, NLT). There is no place I'd rather be than in the presence of Jesus Christ for eternity where I will get to enjoy Him and glorify Him forever and ever. How about you?

Who Do You Say Jesus Is?

God's deep desire is for everyone to come to repentance so that He can spend eternity with us, the crown of His creation. He created us to love us for all of eternity. He sent His Son to die in our place, unquestionably demonstrating just how much He loves us. He wants us to love Him in return, and to make Him known to an unbelieving world.

The most important question ever asked of mankind is very straightforward—who is Jesus Christ? It is a fill-in-the-blank question with only one right answer—mankind's Lord and Savior. Our response to this question literally determines our eternal destiny. Needless to say, it behooves us to respond with the right answer.

When we physically die, one of two scenarios will play out. Either we will try to provide our own meager defense of why we didn't believe and serve Him, and we will have Jesus as our Judge, or Jesus will be our Defender and Savior against *any* accusations. Fortunately, it is very easy to find the answer that will make sure we enjoy the second scenario. The answer is found in the Bible, in the book of Matthew:

> When Jesus came to the region of Caesarea Philippi, he asked his disciples, "Who do people say the Son of Man is?" They replied, "Some say John the Baptist; others say Elijah; and still others, Jeremiah or one of the prophets." "But what about you?" he asked. "Who do you say I am?" Simon Peter answered, "You are the Christ, the Son of the living God." Jesus replied, "Blessed are you, Simon son of Jonah, for this was not revealed to you by man, but by my Father in heaven."
>
> —Matthew 7:13–17

The apostle Paul expounded on the Holy Spirit's work in us when he wrote,

> You know that when you were heathen, you were led off after idols that could not speak [habitually] as impulse directed and whenever the occasion might arise. Therefore I want you to understand that no one speaking under the power and influence of the [Holy] Spirit of God can [ever] say, Jesus be cursed! And no one can [really] say, Jesus is [my] Lord, except by and under the power and influence of the Holy Spirit.
>
> —1 Corinthians 12:2–3, AMP

God reveals Himself to us through His Spirit: "But I will send you the Advocate—the Spirit of truth [Holy Spirit]. He will come to you from the Father and will testify all about me" (John 15:26, NLT). "And when he [the Holy Spirit] comes, he will convict the world of its sin, and of God's righteousness, and of the coming judgment. The world's sin is that it refuses to believe in me [Jesus]" (John 16:8-9, NLT). We have the choice as to whether to respond or not to where the Holy Spirit is leading us.

Either Jesus is who He says He is (Lord), or He is a raving lunatic, or He is a liar of epic proportions. History proves Him to be who He says he is. In addition to the Bible, the Talmud (a collection of books and commentary compiled by Jewish rabbis from A.D. 250–500), the historical writings of Josephus, and numerous other non-Christian writers mentioned miracles He performed and His resurrection (witnessed by over 500 people according to Scripture).

Claiming to be God,[12] Jesus died a horrific death on the Cross for people who mocked, insulted, hated, tormented, tortured, and eventually murdered Him. He died for murderers, cheats, adulterers, prostitutes, homosexuals, liars, idolaters, and thieves (i.e., all of us[13]). Who in their right mind could or would even think to do this, let alone follow through with it? Did anyone else throughout history lay down his or her life for all of us, and then defeat death? No one but Jesus Christ did that.

Make no mistake about it: God has clearly revealed Himself in Jesus Christ. Jesus is the exact representation of God: "The Son is the radiance of God's glory and the exact representation of his being, sustaining all things by his powerful word" (Heb. 1:3a), and: "in Christ lives all the fullness of God in a human body" (Col. 2:9, NLT).

You alone have to decide who you say Jesus is; your parents, siblings, spouse, or friends cannot make this decision for you. Your decision alone will determine how and where you spend eternity. You will spend it in either heaven or hell. This, then, is without a doubt the most important decision you will ever make, because you will live with the consequences of your decision forever.

It is absolutely amazing (tragic, actually) how many people spend more time planning a vacation, shopping for a home or a car, deciding where to go to dinner, or planning for retirement than they will spend seriously thinking or caring about what happens to them after they die.

The Most Important Prayer

The most important prayer comes from your innermost being or spirit, commonly referred to as your "heart," when God the Father opens your spiritual eyes to the realization of who Jesus is and why you need a Savior.

It is a prayer of faith (acting on what you believe), sometimes called "the sinner's prayer." It is your acceptance of the free gift of God's grace, His call (invitation) to come into your life when you realize that only Jesus Christ can save you from the condemnation all of us deserve. The prayer itself, of course, doesn't save you, God's grace saves you. *The faith you have to pray it* saves you when it's prayed as an act of your own will, because you are receiving God's free gift of salvation. Here is an example:

Heavenly Father, I come to You in Jesus' name. I now recognize that I have not lived my life for You up until now. I need You and I want You in my life. I acknowledge that You have completely paid for my sins when Your Son, Jesus Christ, sacrificed His life for me on the Cross. Jesus' sacrifice saved me from the punishment of sin, and His resurrection from the dead assures me of eternal life. Please forgive me for all of my sins. I now turn from them and turn to You. Come into my life right now, Lord Jesus. I give You myself, I belong to You. I will follow You all the rest of the days of my life. Those days are in Your hands. Thank You, Father, for the wonderful gift of salvation. In Jesus' name. Amen.

Heaven Rejoiced

All of the angels in heaven rejoiced when you gave your heart to the Lord Jesus. "I tell you, there is rejoicing in the presence of the angels of God over one sinner who repents" (Luke 15:10). Your next step is to find a church where Jesus Christ is lifted up and the Bible is preached and taught as the inspired and inerrant Word of God. Enroll in a new believer's class and begin to read your Bible (see chapter 9).

All new believers are directed to:

Repent (change your views and purpose to accept the will of God in your inner selves instead of rejecting it) and be baptized, every one of you, in the name of Jesus Christ for the forgiveness of and release from your sins; and you shall receive the gift of the Holy Spirit.

—Acts 2:38, AMP

Being baptized isn't a requirement to be saved. The thief who died on the cross next to Jesus wasn't baptized when he came to a saving faith before he died (Luke 23:40–43). However, it is God's desire that we are baptized. That's good enough for me. I was baptized as a small child, but was baptized again after I came to a saving faith.

The act of baptism is a visible confirmation on your part that you have made a commitment to Jesus Christ. Stepping into the water means that you identify with Christ as He did with you, that you have been washed clean of your sins by His shed blood. Going under the water is a reminder that you have died with Christ, it is no longer you who lives, but Christ who lives in you.[14] As you are raised up out of the water and you step out, you know you have a new, resurrected life; Christ now lives in and through you.

Have you been baptized since you came to a saving faith?

Hopefully this most important prayer will be the beginning of a phenomenal adventure for you. Sadly, for a lot of people who pray this prayer, their lives remain pretty much the same. Far too many Christians who receive Christ never grow into spiritual maturity.

I was one of these Christians. I was on fire for a short time, and then I fell away. I was convicted of my sin and knew I needed salvation. But after I asked Jesus into my life, I got caught up in pretty much the same life I had been living. I didn't really know what it meant to be a Christian or how to live a life that would be pleasing to God. I just knew I needed forgiveness for my sins. I can personally attest to the need to get into a Bible-teaching church and a new believer's class where you can develop a firm foundation in the Word,[15] and come to know and develop relationships with other believers.

The apostle Paul addressed how important this is when he wrote,

> Dear brothers and sisters, when I was with you I couldn't talk to you as I would to spiritual people. I had to talk as though you belonged to this world or as though you were infants in the Christian life. I had to feed you with milk, not with solid food, because you weren't ready for anything stronger. And you still aren't ready, for you are still controlled by your sinful nature. You are jealous of one another and quarrel with each other. Doesn't that prove you are controlled by your sinful nature? Aren't you living like people of the world?
>
> —1 Corinthians 3:1–3, NLT

I am so very thankful that God never gave up on me. He is patient, compassionate, and *always* faithful. He will never give up on you, either!

Amazing Love

God is love.[16] His love for us has no boundaries. God showed us what love is when Jesus laid down His life for us.[17] Jesus' entire life showed us how much God loves us and how much He wants us to know Him and make Him known. God specifically created us to love us, and He longs for us to love Him in return. It's the very reason we were created. That is why life is such a precious gift.

Do you love God? Here is the test. Jesus said, "If you love me, you will obey what I command" (John 14:15). Where do you stand?

Let Me Tell You My Story...

When a high school friend of mine passed away unexpectedly, it gave me the opportunity to share a testimony letter the Holy Spirit had put on my heart to write a few years earlier. I use it to witness to friends, family, coworkers and acquaintances, some of whom I hadn't seen for years, and quite possibly won't see again.

Witnessing is a privilege and an honor because we get to represent the awesome God who saved us. It is also God's expectation of us. It can seem scary and intimidating, but God even gives us everything we need to do it: "But you shall receive power (ability, efficiency, and might) when the Holy Spirit has come upon you, and you shall be My witnesses in Jerusalem and all Judea and Samaria and to the ends (the very bounds) of the earth" (Acts 1:8, AMP).

It can be unsettling, however, to address people face to face with the Good News—for several reasons. Fear is my biggest obstacle. Although I will witness in person whenever I have the opportunity (always ask the Holy Spirit for boldness and the right words), I have found that it is very easy to share my testimony electronically or in printed form (in Christmas, birthday, or get-well cards; with a book, movie or Bible tract, etc.).

A great benefit of sharing the Gospel in a letter, Bible tract, or the like is that the recipients can refer to it when it's convenient for them, and refer back to it whenever they want. It's easy for the deliverer because there is no embarrassment or rejection, the recipients don't argue back, the letter can get right to the point, no speaking skills are required, and you can reach people whom you never thought possible via email, a tract in a bill payment, etc. A relatively recent phenomenon that God has given us is social and professional networking websites (MySpace, Facebook, Twitter, LinkedIn, Plaxo, and others). Our job is to "be prepared in season and out of season" (2 Tim. 4:2), and then to pray fervently that the Holy Spirit will open those individuals' eyes to the need for, and the truth of salvation in Christ.

In 1 Corinthians 3:6 the apostle Paul said, "I planted the seed, Apollos watered it, but God made it grow." You may never hear back about your letter, tract, book, movie, or whatever else from the receiver, but rest assured that you have planted an incorruptible seed—or watered one that has already planted. God just might make them grow! "Let us not become weary in doing good, for at the proper time we will reap a harvest if we do not give up" (Gal. 6:9).

The final results are in God's hands, which is exactly where we want them to be. I am learning to not focus on the work that needs to be done or the imagined enormity of the task. I try to focus on the value of the harvest. And as I was reminded again recently, God builds His kingdom one person at a time. (Please see chapter 9, *Recommended Resources*, section for more information.)

Do you see how easy it can be to share your faith?

My Testimony Letter

I just received the news that Bob has died. It's always hard to say goodbye to someone we know. I remember Bob's great smile.

It's times like this when we all have to ask ourselves the question: where will I be if I don't wake up tomorrow? I know where I'll be. I believe Bob is already there. There is only one way to get there, regardless of what our "enlightened" society tells us.

I have become a devoted follower of Jesus Christ. Let me tell you my story.

I actually accepted Jesus as my Lord and Savior when I was in high school (through Young Life). But the pleasures of seeking my own gratification seemed much more fun. I never developed a personal relationship with Him. I chose to continue to indulge myself.

My dad passed away in October of 1998. My wife and I decided to take my stepmom to church for the Christmas Eve service that year. There I was, celebrating Christmas—the birth of Jesus, our Lord and Savior—in church, without really knowing who He really was or what He had done for me.

We all need a Savior. Why? Because, "All have sinned and fall short of the glory of God" (Rom. 3:23). Have you ever lied, even once? Have you ever stolen anything (the value is irrelevant)? Have you ever taken the Lord's name in vain? If you have looked at someone lustfully, you have committed adultery (Matt. 5:28). If we lie on Monday, we are still liars on Friday. We are all sinners.

It's not a hopeless situation, however. We just need to be redeemed, forgiven, and saved.

After my father's death, I started to go to church on a regular basis, and God started working in my life. He started changing me in ways I never imagined. I began to willingly surrender to Him. Over time, He began to free me from a life of lust, the love of money, pride, anger, fear, doubt, substance abuse, envy, self-centeredness, lack of direction, an over-inflated sense of self, and on and on. "Therefore, if anyone is in Christ, he is a new creation; the old has gone, the new has come!" (2 Cor. 5:17). If we let Him, God changes us from the inside out.

As I began to study the Bible and to know other Christians, I began to experience a multitude of life-changing things. I chose to no longer indulge myself (the "old man," my old nature) and my desires. I have been freed from the hold these things had on me:

> THEREFORE, [there is] now no condemnation (no adjudging guilty of wrong) for those who are in Christ Jesus, who live [and] walk not after the dictates of the flesh, but after the dictates of the Spirit. For the law of the Spirit of life [which is] in Christ Jesus [the law of our new being] has freed me from the law of sin and of death.
> —Romans 8:1–2, AMP

Through Jesus there is complete forgiveness of all sins: "If we confess our sins, he is faithful and just and will forgive us our sins and purify us from all unrighteousness" (1 John 1:9).

It took some time and, yes, I still struggle with the "old man," but he no longer has control of me. Every day I am becoming more and more of the man Jesus had in mind as He was dying on the Cross. I have discovered that a real man is the man who has the courage and conviction to humble himself and willingly follow Jesus Christ.

Death has taken on a new meaning and reality for me. The facts are irrefutable: 1 out of every 1 of us will die. There will probably be at least three things on our tombstone—our name, birth date, and the date we died. All of us will spend much more time dead (physically) than alive.

I know I'll be with Jesus in heaven. Jesus said,

> Do not let your hearts be troubled. Trust in God; trust also in me. In my Father's house are many rooms; if it were not so, I would have told you. I am going there to prepare a place for you. And if I go and prepare a place for you, I will come back and take you to be with me that you also may be where I am.
>
> —John 14:1–3

Are you 100 percent sure you'll be in heaven?

The question I had to ask myself was, "How can I be sure that what Jesus said was true?" Here is what I learned. Jesus was God in the flesh (incarnate): "For to us a child is born, to us a son is given, and the government will be on his shoulders. And he will be called Wonderful, Counselor, Mighty God, Everlasting Father, Prince of Peace" (Isa. 9:6). Also, John 1:1–2, 14 states, "In the beginning was the Word, and the Word was with God, and the Word was God. He was with God in the beginning....The Word became flesh and made his dwelling among us."

He came to earth for our salvation, paying for our sins (as our substitute): "But God demonstrates his own love for us in this: While we were still sinners, Christ died for us" (Rom. 5:8). When He was resurrected, He defeated death, so we have eternal life through Him: "Jesus said ..., 'I am the resurrection and the life. He who believes in me will live, even though he dies; and whoever lives and believes in me will never die....'" (John 11:25–26).

The Bible tells us He is in heaven, at the right hand of the Father. I know where I'm going. What about you? We can be in heaven together!

How do I know the Bible is true? This is a question you must ask. There are many religions and "holy" books in existence. Here is what convinced me.

The Bible consists of sixty-six "books" written over 1,500 years by over forty different authors—all in agreement! Can you imagine even five people in a room completely agreeing about anything? The Bible is proven to be 100 percent historically accurate and backed up by more than 25,000 archeological finds relating to people, places, and events mentioned in its pages (not one has contradicted the Scriptures). If the historical and archeological information is

100 percent accurate, why wouldn't the spiritual part be?

When the Bible was written, about 25 percent of its content predicted future events (prophecy). All of this prophecy has been fulfilled to the minutest detail, except the few remaining prophecies about the return of Jesus Christ. The Bible is true, and the God of the Bible is the only true God: "But the LORD is the only true God, the living God. He is the everlasting King!" (Jer. 10:10).

History (the Talmud, the writings of Josephus, and numerous other writings aside from the Bible) refer to miracles Jesus performed and His resurrection from the dead, which was witnessed by over five hundred people according to Scripture. Jesus, then, is who He claims to be.

In John 14:6, Jesus states, "I am the way and the truth and the life. No one comes to the Father except through me." The proof is overwhelming; there is a God who loves you: "Greater love has no one than this, that he lay down his life for his friends" (John 15:13). He wants a personal relationship with you that will last forever: "For God so loved the world that he gave his one and only Son, that whoever believes in him shall not perish but have eternal life" (John 3:16).

Salvation is God's free gift to us, the chance to spend eternity with Him. Our only other alternative is terrifying.

> Then I saw a great white throne and him who was seated on it. Earth and sky fled from his presence,

and there was no place for them. And I saw the dead, great and small, standing before the throne, and books were opened. Another book was opened, which is the book of life. The dead were judged according to what they had done as recorded in the books. The sea gave up the dead that were in it, and death and Hades gave up the dead that were in them, and each person was judged according to what he had done. Then death and Hades were thrown into the lake of fire. The lake of fire is the second death. If anyone's name was not found written in the book of life, he was thrown into the lake of fire.

—Revelation 20:11–15

How can I know that my name is written in the book? It's written there when you receive Jesus Christ as your Lord.

Satan's goal is to take us to hell with him. Our choice, it would seem, is easy, isn't it? God doesn't *send* anyone to hell, but He will honor our choice to go there if we reject Him.

The only sin God doesn't forgive is the sin of neglect—of not unbelieving in (i.e., rejecting) Jesus Christ. "And to whom was God speaking when he vowed that they would never enter his place of rest? He was speaking to those who disobeyed him. So we see that they were not allowed to enter his rest because of their unbelief" (Heb. 3:18–19).

Again in John 3:17–18,

For God did not send His Son into the world to condemn the world, but to save the world through

Him. Whoever believes in Him is not condemned, but whoever does not believe stands condemned already because he has not believed in the name of God's one and only Son.

It matters that we believe and accept the real truth. Half-truths and outright lies won't get you to heaven. How are you forgiven, and how do you receive eternal life? God made this very clear in the Bible; believe and accept Jesus as your Lord and Savior by faith.

> That if you confess with your mouth, "Jesus is Lord," and believe in your heart that God raised him from the dead, you will be saved. For it is with your heart that you believe and are justified, and it is with your mouth that you confess and are saved.
>
> —Romans 10:9–10

You can receive salvation by faith, by asking Jesus Christ into your life. If you prayed the most important prayer (at the beginning of the chapter[18]) and received Christ into your heart (by faith), welcome to God's family! You have received God's gift of eternal life.

> God saved you by his grace when you believed. And you can't take credit for this; it is a gift from God. Salvation is not a reward for the good things we have done, so none of us can boast about it. For we are God's masterpiece, created anew in Christ Jesus, so that we can do the good things he planned for us long ago.
>
> —Ephesians 2:8–10, NLT

Salvation is God's free gift, but you have to accept it through faith in Jesus Christ. We can't earn our way to heaven, no matter how good we think we are. Jesus is the only way. God will mold and shape you into the person He created you to be, and He will make Himself known to you. Just ask Him. You will never regret it!

Where will you be if you don't wake up tomorrow? My hope and prayer is that we will spend eternity together in the presence of Almighty God. What a joy and blessing that would be!

Share Your Testimony

This is my testimony letter. What's yours? How will your friends and loved ones ever know about salvation through Jesus unless you tell them? The apostle Paul summed it up well when he wrote, "But how can they call on him to save them unless they believe in him? And how can they believe in him if they have never heard about him? And how can they hear about him unless someone tells them?" (Rom. 10:14, NLT).

Write out your own letter or use whatever portions of mine you want (it can be downloaded at www. TheSecondMostImportantPrayer.com). Share it with friends, current and former workplace associates, relatives, high school and college friends, acquaintances, people you meet on social and business networking websites, neighbors, etc. As I previously mentioned, email works really well, or put a hardcopy in Christmas, birthday, or get-well cards, a book, or gift, or anything else you might want to give. Remember that someone witnessed to Mother Teresa, Billy Graham, Dwight L. Moody, and you. (There are additional suggestions on how to witness in Chapter 9.)

> But now God has shown us a way to be made right with him without keeping the requirements of the law, as was promised in the writings of Moses and the prophets long ago. We are made right with God by placing our faith in Jesus Christ. And this is true for everyone who believes, no matter who we are. For everyone has sinned; we all fall short of God's glorious standard. Yet God, with undeserved kindness, declares that we are righteous. He did this through Christ Jesus when he freed us from the penalty for our sins.
>
> —Romans 3:21–24, NLT

Chapter 2

Justification

BEING JUSTIFIED, WE are saved from the punishment of sin through the perfect sacrifice of Jesus Christ (propitiation). God has declared us not guilty. We can have a clear conscience that has been cleansed from guilt and shame by the blood of Jesus Christ. We are now free to live a life that is pleasing to God, because peace, fellowship, and friendship have been restored.

> Since we have now been justified by his blood, how much more shall we be saved from God's wrath through him! For if, when we were God's enemies, we were reconciled to him through the death of his Son, how much more, having been reconciled, shall we be saved through his life! Not only is this so, but we also rejoice in God through our Lord Jesus Christ, through whom we have now received reconciliation.
>
> —Romans 5:9–11

Better Promises

The New Covenant (New Testament) is a "better covenant…established on better promises" (Heb. 8:6). It rests directly on the sacrificial and redemptive work of Christ, the work God accomplished through Him. The Old Covenant (Old Testament) was based on obeying the law given to Moses. It emphasized what Israel was required to do.

God gave us the law, knowing we couldn't keep it, to show us that we need a Savior (the entire Old Testament points to Jesus Christ). "For what the law was powerless to do in that it was weakened by the sinful nature, God did by sending his own Son in the likeness of sinful man to be a sin offering" (Rom. 8:3).

No one could keep the law, except Jesus Himself. Why? Because He never sinned.[1] The New Covenant states what God will do. It was activated by the work of Christ on the Cross, making the Old Covenant obsolete. The New Covenant accomplished what the Old could never do: It cleansed us from sin and a guilty conscience once and for all.[2] All the more reason that the Lord God Almighty deserves all praise, honor, and glory!

Christ's death on the Cross demonstrates His love for us and His commitment to unconditionally forgive us. Saved people are forgiven, saved from God's coming wrath and given eternal life[3] through the shed blood of Christ. Why His shed blood? Because God requires it: "For the life of a creature is in the blood, and I have given it to you to make atonement for yourselves on the altar; it is the blood that makes atonement for one's life" (Lev. 17:11).

Christ's once-for-all sacrifice guaranteed us eternal life,

> For Christ did not enter a man-made sanctuary that was only a copy of the true one; he entered heaven itself, now to appear for us in God's presence. Nor did he enter heaven to offer himself again and again, the way the high priest enters the Most Holy Place every year with blood that is not his own. Then Christ would have had to suffer many times since the creation of the world. But now he has appeared once for all at the end of the ages to do away with sin by the sacrifice of himself.
> —Hebrews 9:24–26

When Jesus died on the Cross, the penalty was paid in full for *every* sin that you or I ever committed or ever will commit. In ancient times, paying a ransom meant a full pardon and release of condemned prisoners. We are no longer condemned and we are free of sin and death![4] Only Jesus Christ, the Son of God, God the Savior ransomed us with His life; Buddha, Confucius, Mohammed, Mary, Lao Tzu, Mahavira, nor anyone else has done what Jesus has done. Only Jesus. Why would you possibly put your faith, trust, and hope for eternal life in anyone else but Him?

Completely Forgiven—Saved from the Punishment of Sin!

"Am I completely forgiven?" you might be asking. It is a difficult concept for most of us to understand and accept. How can this be? There must be some kind of catch.

There are three conditions that must be met in order for God to forgive sin. First, a substitute (sacrifice) has to die in place of the sinner (substitutionary atonement). The Bible says, "God made him who had no sin to be sin for us, so that in him we might become the righteousness of God" (1 Cor. 5:21). Second, the sinner must believe in and receive Jesus Christ. The Bible states, "To Him (Jesus) all the prophets testify (bear witness) that everyone who believes in Him [who adheres to, trusts in, and relies on Him, giving himself up to Him] receives forgiveness of sins through His name" (Acts 10:43, AMP). And third, we confess.

> If we [freely] admit that we have sinned and confess our sins, He is faithful and just (true to His own nature and promises) and will forgive our sins [dismiss our lawlessness] and [continuously] cleanse us from all unrighteousness [everything not in conformity to His will in purpose, thought, and action].
> —1 John 1:9, AMP

Jesus is described in the book of Hebrews as "the Mediator of the New Covenant" (Heb. 9:15). Hebrews 9:15 goes on to tell us "that those who are called may receive the promised eternal inheritance—now that he has died as a ransom to set them free from the sins committed under the first covenant."

Get it completely settled in your mind that when we inherit salvation, we are completely and unconditionally forgiven and accepted by God through Jesus Christ. Every sin we have ever committed or will commit has been paid for by Christ's death on the Cross. God's grace (unmerited favor) was unconditional the moment we placed our faith in Jesus Christ. Please note that good, nice, well-intentioned, cute, funny, caring, witty, religious, happy, positive people don't inherent salvation; only forgiven people do.

We learned in chapter 1 that sin (missing the mark) deserves God's punishment and incurs His wrath because it is a violation of His holy character. Formerly separated from a holy God because of our sin, we have now been reconciled through Christ. Praise God that He forgives and forgets. His merciful pardon is unconditional!

We are justified by putting our faith in Jesus Christ.[5] Not faith plus works, tithing, Bible study, fellowship, worship, prayer. Just faith. Everything else happens because of our gratitude toward God because of what He has, is, and will do for us. Being justified is the beginning of the magnificent journey of salvation where "you died to this life, and your real life is hidden with Christ in God" (Col. 3:3, NLT).

God now looks at us just as if we had never sinned! We have been saved from the punishment of sin, having been washed completely clean by the shed blood of Christ on the Cross.[6] Justification is our position in Christ. It is a one-time occurrence. Most followers of Christ call this "being saved."

As we saw in chapter 1, we are actually being saved, and will be saved every day throughout eternity. We are currently saved from the power of sin, or sanctification. In the future, we will be saved from the very presence of sin, or glorification. Phenomenal!

God promises us that our past is not only forgiven, but that our sins are completely forgotten. Through the prophet Isaiah, God told us, "I, even I, am he who blots out your transgressions, for my own sake, and remembers your sins no more" (Isa. 43:25). This is why the Gospel is the Good News, and why the Lord God Almighty deserves all praise, honor, and glory!

God Will Welcome You Back

I thought I had it made. Life was good from my perspective. I was living a comfortable lifestyle with a great wife, wonderful children, and a promising career. I felt that I "knew" God. I just didn't need to go to church, read the Bible, or be involved in other "Christian" activities. I thought that I could worship Him in my own way. That lie lasted for about thirty years. I was blissfully blind to the truth about God's love, grace, mercy, faithfulness, patience, and judgment because I chose to be.

You see, I never thought about my salvation, never thanked God for His abundant blessings, and wasn't concerned about the self-centered choices I was making in a lot of areas of my life, because I really didn't know anything about Him. I watched pro football games for years seeing the John 3:16 signs that were often held up in the end zone seats during the extra point attempts, not even realizing what John 3:16 was. I used His holy name as a swear word just to appear tough and cool with my worldly friends.

But something was wrong. Something was definitely missing; I just didn't know what it was. There was anger and frustration just below the surface, and pride was a big part of my life. There was also a part of me that was empty (my spirit had atrophied). I didn't realize that my spirit was comatose because I was away from the True Vine—Jesus.[7] I was frustrated with job politics and bickering. I was very impatient. I was short-tempered with my family. One day my daughter wrote me a note expressing concern that I seemed angry a lot. My response was, "I am *not* angry!"

I remember thinking about how I just needed to get the right self-help book or go to the right seminar. I felt that I just needed a different focus. I wasn't quite ready to see that the only thing worth focusing on is Jesus Christ: "Let us fix our eyes on Jesus, the author and perfecter of our faith..." (Heb. 12:2). I was still in a spiritual pigpen.

Perhaps like you, I was a poster child as the prodigal son (Luke 15:11–32). As I mentioned, the Lord called (invited) me at sixteen or seventeen (in *Young Life*), asking if I would let Him come into my life and be my Lord and receive Him as my Savior. I got down on my knees one night and asked Him into my life, gladly accepting the inheritance (eternal life) that Jesus purchased for me. But I was joined at the hip with the world (unbelievers). I knew I needed a Savior, but I didn't know how to "unplug" from my former life as an unbeliever and follow Him. And, to be honest, I didn't really try that hard. I rapidly drifted back to my "old" life, ignorantly unaware that friendship with the world (not having friends who are unbelievers, but blending in with and embracing what they do) is hatred toward

God.[8] I was dishonoring my heavenly Father, my Savior, my Advocate, Counselor and Teacher.

God's plan is for all of His children to meet together frequently (in addition to weekly church services). Fellowship—meeting, learning, and sharing with other Christians (mostly with your same gender unless you are in a couples small home-growth group or Bible study), is absolutely essential. (More on this in Chapter 5.) So is being in Bible study, various biblically based men's and women's ministries, etc. All Christians need to be involved, learning, serving and growing with other Christians. The Bible says,

> "Let us think of ways to motivate one another to acts of love and good works. And let us not neglect our meeting together, as some people do, but encourage one another, especially now that the day of his return is drawing near."
>
> —Hebrews 10:24–25, NLT

Fellowship is so important because we are all in God's family. We can encourage one another, lift each other up in prayer, walk along side those who are hurting, learn from each other, etc.

I wasn't involved in any type of fellowship. I was way more interested in my girlfriend. I subsequently ended up with virtually no foundation in Christ. I just went on doing what I wanted to do, whenever I wanted to do it, comfortable in my own ignorance.

Thirty years later, being in my self-made spiritual pigpen became intolerable. I came to a point (actually God brought me there, giving me the choice as to how I wanted to proceed) in my life where I was sick and tired of being sick and tired. Pent-up anger, ego, stubbornness, despair, frustration, and a feeling of helplessness with no spiritual direction eventually pushed me into a corner.

God Draws Near

The Holy Spirit kept lovingly but firmly convicting me of my brokenness, and life's circumstances kept pointing out how empty I was in so many areas of my life. As I started to see God at work in my life, I was convicted that being lukewarm in my walk was the worst possible scenario—half in, half out. One time I was listening to my pastor's sermon. I can't even remember what he was saying, but I knew that it was God speaking directly to me. God was undeniably getting my attention. I was beginning to taste and see that God is good.[9]

But I continued holding tightly to the junk and trash I had been dragging around for years because I was afraid to let it go. It was all I knew. One time during my lukewarm period my wife asked me if I wanted a divorce. It wasn't because she wanted one, but she thought I did because of the way I was acting. Here I was thinking that I was walking on the right path with God. But I was still burdened by being angry, unforgiving, egotistical, and prideful, and I was generally unhappy about how inadequate I was at doing most things consistently well. But I never thought *I* was the problem. It was always circumstances and other people; if only this would happen, if only I could do that, why can't they understand?

God was (and still is) doing a good work in me,[10] which includes showing me how broken I am in so many areas and how much I need Him. He did this because He loves me. He has a much better plan for me than I could even begin to imagine. He has the same thing in mind for you.

We all tend to make a pretty big mess of things on our own. In 2000 I bought a brand new, fire engine red Mustang GT convertible with all of the trimmings, just as God was just starting to get my attention again. For good measure, I added a two-chamber free flow exhaust and a high-performance air filter. This car needed to be driven fast, I rationalized. So that's what I did. I also rationalized that it was one of the nicest cars on the road, so guess what happened to my pride?

During that time I was convicted to go to a men's retreat with my church. My attitude towards retreats was, "Who wants to go to a mountain retreat with a bunch of guys I don't really know with everything I have to do?" God had other plans. Right after a testimony in church in which they were urging men to sign up for the retreat, my wife nudged me and asked if I was planning on going. I wasn't sure if it was a suggestion or a directive, but it was just what I needed.

During the first night of that retreat I was in a cabin with my roommates. We starting talking about burdens we were carrying. I was having a lot of conflict with my boss's boss. After I explained the problems, one of the guys just looked at me and said, "Have you prayed for him?" That really got my attention as I hadn't even considered that. Here was God speaking to me in the middle of the Santa Cruz Mountains with several guys I didn't know. Our God *is* an awesome God!

It takes time for God to lovingly reveal our brokenness so He can begin to heal us. It takes even more time for us to realize just how broken we really are and just how much we need God in every detail of our lives. Sadly, many Christians never come to this point, most often because of pride. But God promises that if we humble ourselves before Him, He will lift us up.[11]

What is most amazing about God in the prodigal son parable (an earthly story with a heavenly meaning) is that when we turn back to God, He immediately comes running to us. There is a celebration in heaven for the son or daughter who was lost, but now is found![12] Are you ready to come out of the pigpen? God has been patiently waiting for you.

Unpack Your Burdens

It's human nature to want to drag around past baggage, things we wish we could and should forget. We think it's our debt to pay: bearing guilt and shame. But God has forgotten about them; He has given us a clean slate.

It took me a couple of years after coming back into my heavenly Father's loving arms to express my sorrow for all of my many transgressions. He had already forgiven me,[13] but I had never told Him how truly sorry I was. Our actual confession is important, as it cleanses us completely (alleviates guilt and shame), and takes us much closer to God.

As I mentioned, I had reluctantly agreed to go to a men's retreat about two years after I began to renew my commitment to Jesus. The retreat leader invited all of us to go off on our own to a quiet place and confess any sins that we hadn't asked God to forgive, that we were holding on to, and to tell God how sorry we are.[14]

I found myself in the middle of a baseball field in the Santa Cruz Mountains (California) with the warm sun on my back. With tears streaming down I said, "Father, I'm so sorry for what I have done. Thank You for forgiving me." I felt like I had just crawled up on my Father's lap and said I was sorry.

I immediately experienced the very presence of God like I had never felt before. His warm and loving embrace confirmed that He appreciated my confession. It was spectacular! He let me know that all had not only been forgiven, but forgotten. The love I felt was immense, all-encompassing, complete. The loving, merciful, mighty, majestic, holy, long-suffering, gracious, all-powerful Creator of the universe was hanging out with me! I can't wait to be in His presence 24/7! How about you?

Jesus leads the way to forgiveness, but you have to be willing to follow. Are you ready right now to lay down your burdens? Jesus Himself said,

> Come to me, all you who are weary and burdened, and I will give you rest. Take my yoke upon you and learn from me, for I am gentle and humble in heart, and you will find rest for your souls. For my yoke is easy and my burden is light.
> —Matthew 11:28–30

Thank You, Lord Jesus, my merciful Savior.

Forgive Yourself

Who is the toughest person to forgive? Oftentimes it's ourselves. Please make sure you have forgiven yourself, because God forgave you. Jesus saw you as someone worth forgiving unconditionally, someone worth dying for. In Hebrews 9:14 we're told, "How much more, then, will the blood of Christ, who through the eternal Spirit offered himself unblemished to God, cleanse our consciences from acts that lead to death, so that we may serve the living God!"

His blood even cleansed us from guilt so that we can be confident in serving Him! That should end any internal turmoil, guilt, or shame you may be feeling—He bought your freedom with His own blood. That is the highest price by far that has ever been paid to ransom anyone, and all because God says you are worth it!

That means it doesn't matter what anyone else may say about you, including you. It doesn't matter what you have done. It only matters what God says about you, and He is madly in love with all of His children. "O Lord, you are so good, so ready to forgive, so full of unfailing love for all who ask for your help" (Ps. 86:5, NLT).

King David wrote, "As far as the east is from the west, so far has he removed our transgressions from us" (Ps. 103:12). If you are traveling east, you will never start traveling west. That's how far! And David definitely knew firsthand about God's forgiveness. We may still have to live with the consequences of our sin, but God does not hold those sins against us; He forgets them. He has completely forgiven and forgotten your past—you have a clean slate!

So be prudent by imitating Him as we are told, "THEREFORE BE imitators of God [copy Him and follow His example], as well-beloved children [imitate their father]" (Eph. 5:1, AMP). However the Bible also says,

> When God our Savior revealed his kindness and love, he saved us, not because of the righteous things we had done, but because of his mercy. He washed away our sins, giving us a new birth and new life through the Holy Spirit. He generously poured out the Spirit upon us through Jesus Christ our Savior. Because of his grace he declared us righteous and gave us confidence that we will inherit eternal life.
>
> —Titus 3:4–7, NLT

Chapter 3

Sanctification

It is not what we do that matters, but what a sovereign God chooses to do through us. God doesn't want our success; He wants us. He doesn't demand our achievements; He demands our obedience. The kingdom of God is a kingdom of paradox, where through the ugly defeat of a cross, a holy God is utterly glorified. Victory comes through defeat; healing through brokenness; finding self through losing self.

—Charles Colson, from his book *Loving God*

I plead with you to give your bodies to God because of all he has done for you. Let them be a living and holy sacrifice—the kind he will find acceptable. This is truly the way to worship him. Don't copy the behavior and customs of this world, but let God transform you into a new person by changing the way

you think. Then you will learn to know God's will
for you, which is good and pleasing and perfect.
—Romans 12:1–2, NLT

At Peace with God

SINCE WE HAVE been saved from the punishment
of sin, we have peace with God. We are no longer
condemned sinners and objects of His wrath.

> But God demonstrates his own love for us in this:
> While we were still sinners, Christ died for us. Since
> we have now been justified by his blood, how much
> more shall we be saved from God's wrath through
> him! For if, when we were God's enemies, we were
> reconciled to him through the death of his Son,
> how much more, having been reconciled, shall we
> be saved through his life!
> —Romans 5:8–10

What an incredible gift!

Sanctification is more than growing in our likeness
of Christ, more than becoming who we already are
in Christ and being set apart to be used by God. It
is the ongoing process of learning to trust Him. We
are not meant to understand everything about God.
How could we? We are meant to trust and follow
Him. He wants us to grow in our knowledge of Him
every day. He wants us to experience Him in every
detail of our lives.[1]

We're Being Saved Every Day

Being saved is not a one-time event. We are being saved every day. Having been saved from the punishment of sin, we are currently being saved from the power of sin (sanctification). We are free to serve God.[2]

We can't allow ourselves to be deceived, however. We can't accept Jesus as our Lord and then go about living a self-centered life, like I did for so many years. We can't imagine that all of our problems will just go away or that nothing will really change. Jesus said, "So why do you keep calling me 'Lord, Lord!' when you don't do what I say?" (Luke 6:46, NLT). Dramatic change starts from the inside out, through the power of the Holy Spirit. We should allow and embrace changes in our lives by allowing the Holy Spirit to lead us because we want to become more and more like Jesus and do what pleases Him.[3]

The perfect nature of Jesus is found in Galatians 5:22–23a: "The fruit of the Spirit is love, joy, peace, patience, kindness, goodness, faithfulness, gentleness, and self-control." Jesus clearly modeled these character traits in His life, death, and resurrection. God will put all of His children in situations (we typically think of them as *trials and tests*) so we can grow in our ability to love unconditionally, experience and share the joy of being a child of God in our hearts, learn and practice self control, learn to trust, and more, on the journey of perfecting us to be like Jesus. Thank You, Father, for loving us that much!

God has really worked with me on developing patience. Like pumping weights in the gym to tone and build muscle mass, He has given me numerous life experiences that have tested and grown my patience. Even though I have failed at times, I continue to see real progress. God tests us to grow us, not to flunk us so that we drop out and give up. Remember, the Holy Spirit is our Advocate, Comforter, and Teacher. And God lovingly reminds me how patient He is and has been with me.

We develop our desire to praise, worship, and serve God because we get to, not because we think we have to (legalism) or that God will be mad at us if we don't. It's not just checking the "I'm saved and have eternal life and fire insurance" box on a list of things to do in our lives and then doing what we always have. If we aren't increasing in spiritual knowledge and maturity daily (the Bible calls it being transformed by the renewing of your mind[4]), we are backsliding (withering spiritually), and dishonoring God by not allowing ourselves to be conformed into the likeness of our Lord, who is preparing us to be in heaven with Him. But God gives us all of the tools we need to grow, starting with His holy Word. We just need to be open and willing to follow so the Holy Spirit can lead us.[5]

Saints Who Sin

It's important to understand that we are now saints (those who call Jesus "Lord" and bear true and faithful witness to Him) who still sin. We aren't just sinners saved by grace; we are saints set apart to be used by God: "But you are a chosen people, a royal priesthood, a holy nation, a people belonging to God, that you may declare the praises of him who called you out of darkness into his wonderful light"(1 Peter 2:9). This is who we are in Christ. Our old nature is dead, but we still react to life through our conditioned responses and learned behaviors, emotions, and self-centered attitudes. In short, we are forgiven sinners.

The challenge we now face is responding to the prompting of the Holy Spirit, who lives is us.[6] The more we respond, the more sin becomes abhorrent to us, and the more we become like Jesus.

Over the years, I have struggled with being an angry driver when I get behind the wheel of a car. Incompetent and dangerous drivers have always been a pet peeve of mine. More times than not I react very angrily when I get cut off, get behind a slow driver in a faster lane, or see speeding drivers weaving in and out of traffic. My conditioned response (because I have done it for so many years) is to yell, shake my head in disbelief, and throw up my hands. Recently I realized the real culprit is pride. How dare they get in my way! How dare they slow me down; I have places to be!

I know this behavior does not glorify God in the least. I have prayed for years to have more grace and mercy behind the wheel of a car. I am so grateful that I am better than I used to be, and some days are great, but I still have a ways to go in this and other sin areas of my life. It is an encouragement and praise that Jesus will give me strength in all things, anytime I need it.[7]

I tell God that I am sorry anytime I do something that doesn't glorify Him. Why? Not because I need to be saved and forgiven again, but because I am truly sorry, and I want my heavenly Father to hear it from me. I may have grieved His Spirit[8] and may possibly be quenching the Holy Spirit's work in me.[9] You may be thinking, "Are we still saved even though we still sin?" Of course! The wonder of Christ's death on the Cross is that He paid for all sins, past, present, and future. One clear sign of obedience and spiritual maturity is not wanting to knowingly sin, and *immediately* asking God's forgiveness even thought we know we are forgiven.

Since I came back to the Lord, I have discovered several fresh insights. As a new creation of God, I don't want to sin. When I get behind the wheel of my car I intentionally remind myself not to do verbal battle. While watching TV, I am very sensitive to the dozens and dozens of shows that glorify sexual immorality, adultery, greed, divorce, idolatry, self-centeredness, etc. I have made a covenant with God to not surf the internet or watch TV to fulfill sexual fantasies: "I made a covenant with my eyes not to look lustfully at a girl" (Job 31:1).

Alcohol is no longer a part of my life. I realize that the Bible doesn't forbid alcohol consumption, but it warns me: "Do not get drunk on wine, which leads to debauchery. Instead, be filled with the Spirit" (Eph. 5:18). I used to drink excessively in college and while in the Navy, which led to totally inappropriate behavior. I want my whole life to be under God's control now. I want to be emptied of me so He can fill me with the Holy Spirit. How about you? What specific sin(s) do you need to lay on the altar? Whatever they are, do it right this moment and let Jesus be your strength. "Yet the Lord is faithful, and He will strengthen [you] and set you on a firm foundation and guard you from the evil [one]" (2 Thess. 3:3, AMP). Then follow Paul's advice:

> Not that I have ... already been made perfect, but I press on to take hold of that for which Christ Jesus took hold of me. Brothers, I do not consider myself yet to have taken hold of it. But one thing I do: Forgetting what is behind and straining toward what is ahead, I press on toward the goal to win the prize for which God has called me heavenward in Christ Jesus.
>
> —Philippians 3:12-14

Set Apart by a Holy God—No Higher Calling

God wants to use His children to make Him known.[10] *Sanctification* is the biblical term used to describe the sinner's process (journey) of becoming who God has called him or her to be. Our old self (nature) was crucified with Christ. We have a brand new nature that God wants to work through: "Put off your old self, which is being corrupted by its deceitful desires; to be made new in the attitude of your minds; and to put on the new self, created to be like God in true righteousness and holiness" (Eph. 4:22-24).

It is the new creation that is holy (set apart), righteous (in right standing with God), pure (morally clean), and blameless (innocent, irreproachable) in God's sight.

God sanctifies all believers when they receive Christ by faith:

> It is God's will that you should be sanctified: that you should avoid sexual immorality; that each of you

should learn to control his own body in a way that
is holy and honorable… For God did not call us to
be impure, but to live a holy life. Therefore, he who
rejects this instruction does not reject man but God,
who gives you his Holy Spirit.

—1 Thessalonians 4:3–4, 7–8

Justification, as we learned, is a one-time occurrence
(chapter 2). It is past tense salvation. Sanctification is
current tense salvation, where God expects our active
participation.[11] And of course God provides everything
we need to be sanctified,[3] including having His Spirit live
in us. It's not what we have or do, but what we allow God
to do in and through us that results in significance.

Diamonds in the Rough

We are totally bombarded by information. So many
pieces of information pass through our brains each day,
it's overwhelming at times. Have you ever had the experience where out of all that is going on, one statement,
one Bible verse, one news item, one comment from a
friend or stranger or whatever hits you right between
the eyes and convicts you to do something? Or do you
find yourself burdened with an injustice, hurting people,
blatant immorality, political corruption, etc.? Is it on
your heart to reconcile with someone?

Several years ago I was talking with a Christian friend
of mine. He told me he came to a saving faith when he
read a Bible tract. The Holy Spirit put it in my spirit right
then to hand out Bible tracts. I learned to put them in
the bills I paid, on gas pumps, around the grocery store,

in the mall, in restrooms, on the driver's side door, etc. You can get good quality tracts for between four cents and fifteen cents each. God may bring a lost soul to Him with a four cent Bible tract (more about this in chapter 9). Talk about a worthwhile eternal investment! Is there something God is urging you to do? Remember, He gives you the desire *and* the power to do what pleases Him.[3]

As God was drawing me back to Himself (my luke-warm phase) after my thirty-year absence, I remember thinking that I didn't really want to do everything that God might want me to do because He may send me to Africa. That thought freaked me out. I have come to realize that God changes our desires as we come to know Him more, and then uses the talent and skills He has given us so we *want to* do what He wants. I also realize that if God wants to send me to Africa, He will give me the desire to do so. I would go not because I felt I had to (legalism), I would go because I want to please Him (obedience).

Because God created us in Christ and set us apart to do good works (we are *all* called to bear witness about Jesus), it behooves us to be about our heavenly Father's business, since, "You also must be ready, because the Son of Man will come at an hour when you do not expect him" (Luke 12:40). Additionally, we should endeavor to glorify God in everything we do: "So whether you eat or drink or whatever you do, do it all for the glory of God" (1 Cor. 10:31).

The way we can glorify Him in whatever we do is to have the right attitude—grateful, humble, obedient, loving, and joyful—because we are thankful to Whom we belong. Ask God to give you the same attitude of Jesus.[12] This is key, because without Jesus we can do nothing.[13]

Several years ago, I was moved to write the following in my journal: "Jesus, before dying on the Cross, had in mind who He wanted me to be. I hereby dedicate every day of my life to being that person." I believe God will tell us what He wants us to do, if we are open to hear, and then follow Him. Are you open to hearing to what God is saying to you?

Trusting God's Word

Renewal of our minds means we have a brand new attitude (gratitude) and new ideals by which we want to live in order to please God. Transforming our minds starts by reading the Bible and doing what it says. "Do not merely listen to the word, and so deceive yourselves. Do what it says" (James 1:22).

A particular Scripture I have learned to live by is Matthew 11:28 (NLT), where Jesus said, "Come to me, all of you who are weary and carry heavy burdens, and I will give you rest." I have relied heavily on this passage dozens of times because God always delivers by giving me the rest He promises.

Once when my daughter was away at college (about sixty miles away), a girlfriend of hers came in from out of town. She had a coupon for an additional free room at her hotel. My daughter went to stay at the hotel, but she had her mobile phone turned off. About forty-eight hours had passed since we had called her. My wife and I started to panic, thinking she was missing. Her friends hadn't heard from her either. I called the campus police, who advised me to meet with them as soon as possible.

On the drive to the school, I had this sense of dread. I was trying to maintain my composure when Matthew 11:28 popped into my head (see also John 14:26). I began asking the Lord Jesus to carry the burden that was crushing me. He did. I began to feel a sense of calm and order (the Holy Spirit is the Comforter). I began to think much more clearly. I got to taste God's supernatural peace![14]

I got to her dorm with an eight-by-ten picture of my daughter. The campus police arrived. About fifteen minutes later, my daughter called. The Holy Spirit had put it on her heart to check in (finally!). It was just after ten p.m. She came through the door about twenty minutes later with what I could only describe as a glow about her. She had given her life to Jesus in the hotel room the night before! This is one of the many encounters with God that paved the way for me to completely give my heart to Him!

God gives us rest and peace, because without it we tend to focus on the chaos and confusion instead of on Him.[15] I learned that I need to be faithful to God by putting my hope in His promises alone. Why? Because He always keeps His promises. What is God teaching you? If you're not sure, ask, listen, and then respond in obedience.

You Died, Now Act Like It

We now know that our old nature, having been crucified with Christ, is dead. Now Christ lives in us[16] through the Holy Spirit. God desires us to be fully engaged in our salvation.

> Therefore, my dear ones, as you have always obeyed [my suggestions], so now, not only [with the enthusiasm you would show] in my presence but much more because I am absent, work out (cultivate, carry out to the goal, and fully complete) your own salvation with reverence and awe and trembling (self-distrust, with serious caution, tenderness of conscience, watchfulness against temptation, timidly shrinking from whatever might offend God and discredit the name of Christ). [Not in your own strength] for it is God Who is all the while effectually at work in you [energizing and creating in you the power and desire], both to will and to work for His good pleasure and satisfaction and delight.
> —Philippians 2:12b–13, AMP

What skills and talents do you have? What do you enjoy doing? Works are taking what God gives you and using those abilities to glorify Him because you want to, and get to please Him. For example, say you really enjoy interacting with people. Be an usher, greeter, Big Brother/Sister, mentor, nursing home volunteer, Bible study host/hostess, etc. If you really like children, teach Sunday school, volunteer in the nursery, or help at a summer camp, vacation Bible school, or crisis pregnancy center. The list of how we can serve others is endless.

We are not saved by doing good works; we are saved by God's grace. We receive His gift of grace by placing our faith in Jesus Christ.[17] We are, however, expected to serve others based on our gifts, both natural (based on your skills, personality, etc.) and supernatural as apportioned by the Holy Spirit. Good works are not the *means to* salvation; only faith in Jesus Christ is. Good works are a *result of* salvation. Our works demonstrate that our faith is genuine.[18]

Jesus said, "It is more blessed to give than to receive" (Acts 20:35). Have you ever done a good deed for someone without expecting or wanting anything in return? Remember how good it felt? Pure joy.

One time I was volunteering at a soup kitchen. A mom came in with her young son. He was probably about ten. A local grocery store had donated a chocolate cake to our kitchen. It was a beautiful cake. The Holy Spirit put it in my heart to walk up to that young man and personally ask if he would like a piece of that cake. His eyes got wide and he said, "Yes, please!"

As I served him while fighting back tears, my spirit was overflowing with the love of Jesus Christ. I had no clue what their circumstances were, but it occurred to me later that maybe God wanted to show them a man who was willing to do something special for them with no strings or expectations attached. Isn't that what Jesus did for us?

I experienced the joy of serving someone unconditionally, and I was humbled that God had used me. What's God calling you to do? Ask Him to use you. He will.

This is the confidence (the assurance, the privilege of boldness) which we have in Him: [we are sure] that if we ask anything (make any request) according to His will (in agreement with His own plan), He listens to and hears us. And if (since) we [positively] know that He listens to us in whatever we ask, we also know [with settled and absolute knowledge] that we have [granted us as our present possessions] the requests made of Him.

—1 John 5:14–15, AMP

God Always Delivers on His Promises

God always keeps His promises.[19] I have learned by countless experiences that God's Word will do what it says:

> For Jesus Christ, the Son of God, does not waver between "Yes" and "No." He is the one whom Silas, Timothy, and I preached to you, and as God's ultimate "Yes," he always does what he says. For all of God's promises have been fulfilled in Christ with a resounding "Yes!"
>
> —2 Corinthians 1:19–20, NLT

Don't you think it's important to understand what those promises are? That's why reading and studying the Bible is essential (more on this in chapter 8). It's not that you have to have all of God's promises memorized; it's that you have to expose yourself to the Word consistently so the Holy Spirit can "teach you all things and will remind you of everything I have said to you" (John 14:26).

I have, for example, pretty much eliminated the word *worry* from my vocabulary. There are so many things that we can choose to worry about, but Scripture says,

> Therefore I tell you, do not worry about your life, what you will eat or drink; or about your body, what you will wear. Is not life more important than food, and the body more important than clothes? Look at the birds of the air; they do not sow or reap or store away in barns, and yet your heavenly Father feeds them. Are you not much more valuable than they? Who of you by worrying can add a single hour to his life?
>
> —Matthew 6:25–27

Worry is taking on a burden God never intended for us to carry because we will obsess on the issues we have absolutely no control over rather than keeping our eyes on Jesus.

When the apostle Peter began to walk on the water, he had his eyes directly on Jesus. But because the wind distracted him, he took his eyes off of Jesus and began to look at his circumstances (sound familiar?). Then he began to sink. But what he did next is the lesson for all of us. He looked back at Jesus and said, "Lord, save me!" Jesus didn't let him sink farther and wallow in his despair; He reached down, caught him, and pulled him up and said, "You of little faith, why did you doubt?" (Matt. 14:25–31). Jesus will help us if we let Him, even when our faith is wavering. He is *always* there for us.[20]

A Grateful Heart

I have come to realize that one of the very few things we can control in our lives is our attitude. Please take a minute to read Psalm 145, a psalm of praise written by King David. God has done *everything* to give us peace with Him and to restore a relationship with us, including putting all of our sin, guilt, and shame on His Son.

When you begin to realize who you are in Christ (a new creation who has been saved and set free from the power of sin) and what He has done and is doing and will do for you, you should begin to develop an attitude of gratitude. Gratitude leads to joy. Joy replaces despair and hopelessness, and the very love of God begins to flow from your heart.[21] Jesus talks about this in John chapter 15:10–12:

> If you obey my commands, you will remain in my love, just as I have obeyed my Father's commands and remain in his love. I have told you this so that my joy may be in you and that your joy may be complete. My command is this: Love each other as I have loved you.

I had a picture in my mind once that if God were an ocean, I'd probably know about a bucket's worth of water about Him. I'm sure it's much more than that (a small lake, maybe?), but hopefully you see my point. God is a *big* God. Way bigger than any problem or circumstance we will ever face.

As I previously mentioned, the Bible is replete with dozens of promises God made and kept. The most notable and incredible one was the promised Messiah who would take away the sins of the world.[22]

We get a few glimpses of what God has in store for His children. In the book of Revelation, the apostle John saw and heard absolutely incredible things. In chapter 21:2–4 (NLT), he writes,

> I saw the holy city, the new Jerusalem, coming down from God out of heaven like a bride beautifully dressed for her husband. I heard a loud shout from the throne, saying, "Look, God's home is now among his people! He will live with them, and they will be his people. God himself will be with them. He will wipe every tear from their eyes, and there will be no more death or sorrow or crying or pain. All these things are gone forever."

I don't know about you, but I can't wait to see this! Can you begin to see why all Christians should be eternally grateful? That we should be filled with joy? An attitude of thankfulness should result in *our active and willing participation in our salvation,* wanting to do what God tells us to do. Every Christian's motto should be, "Holy Spirit, You lead, I'll follow."

King David wrote: "Teach me to do your will, for you are my God. May your gracious Spirit lead me forward on a firm footing" (Ps. 143:10, NLT). Are you willing to follow where the Holy Spirit is leading you?

God Is Better than Ice Cream

Remember the potato chip commercial with the tagline, "I bet you can't eat just one"? I have never been able to eat just one potato chip or just one spoonful of ice cream. Have you? Tasting Jesus in your life leaves you with a desire to know Him more and to be more like Him.

> Blessed and fortunate and happy and spiritually prosperous (in that state in which the born-again child of God enjoys His favor and salvation) are those who hunger and thirst for righteousness (uprightness and right standing with God), for they shall be completely satisfied!
> —Matthew 5:6, AMP

I absolutely love ice cream. I would eat it every day if I could, but my bad cholesterol would go through the roof, not to mention my weight. One of my goals in life is to come to the point where I can eat ice cream every day and not be concerned about it. I'm not sure if that day will ever come, though, and I'm OK if it doesn't. I know there is something so much better in heaven anyway!

Besides, I like knowing and experiencing God way more than ice cream. I like experiencing Him in my life and in the lives of those around me more than anything. The closer I come to Him in my quiet time, prayer, reading Scripture, fellowship, hanging out with my wife, children, others, hiking, enjoying a beautiful sunset, etc., the more I crave closer fellowship with Him. And He becomes much more familiar to me. Jesus is absolutely irresistible!

Just like ice cream for me, once you taste of Him (experience Him in your life) you want more and more. It's impossible to do anything in your life but love, submit, obey, and be humble with an attitude of gratitude when you continually taste the Lord. How? Make yourself continuously available. "Then Jesus said to his disciples, 'If anyone would come after me, he must deny himself and take up his cross and follow me'" (Matt. 16:24).

One time I chewed some zinc tablets at the onset of a cold. I lost my sense of taste for several hours. Sometimes our spiritual taste buds have become dulled by circumstances, and we forget how good God is. How do we "wake up" our spirit? Find a church where Christ is lifted up and the Bible is taught (pray about this). Join or rejoin a recommended Bible study and/or small group (it may not be part of your church), and then put into practice what you learn. Read the book of First John seven days in a row, so you can refresh your memory on God's love for His children and the assurance of eternal life. Ask God to rejuvenate your spiritual taste buds. Are you ready?

When we start to "let go and let God," we begin to get a different perspective about Him. We begin to recognize Him in our lives. The more we come to know Jesus, the more we learn to trust and depend on Him. The more we trust and depend on Him, the more grateful we become because we begin to see His fingerprints in all aspect of our lives. I am completely grateful for whom Jesus is and the work He has done, is doing, and will do in me. A grateful heart wants to serve, honor, obey and praise the one True God,[23] who alone is worthy of all praise, honor, and glory!

God is so good that once you begin to experience Him, you can *never* get enough! Halleluiah! "I will exalt you, my God and King, and praise your name forever and ever. I will praise you every day; yes, I will praise you forever. Great is the LORD! He is most worthy of praise! No one can measure his greatness" (Ps. 145:1–3, NLT).

Chapter 4

Biblical Worldview

Our lives will change dramatically when we stop worshiping the false god(s) we created in our imaginations, and start actively seeking and worshiping the God Who created us.

—Patrick Morley, author's paraphrase

Christianity is unique in that it claims that instead of people working to gain access to God, God has made Himself known to people. His ultimate self-disclosure was in Jesus Christ. No longer is He the unknown God. Although "no one has seen God at any time," Jesus "has declared Him" (John 1:18). So does Christianity claim that all other religions are totally wrong? Of course not. Most have some measure of truth in them. Islam and Judaism in particular have a great deal of truth in them. They are like candles that bring a bit of light into a very

dark world. Nevertheless, all religions pale into insignificance at the dawn that has come with Christ. He fulfills the hopes, the aspirations, the virtues, and the insights of whatever is true and good in all faiths.
—*Word in Life Study Bible*. 1997, c1996.
Nashville: Thomas Nelson electronic ed.,
see Acts 4:31

Living the Life

WHAT IS A biblical worldview? A biblical worldview is seeing life, past, present and future as it pertains to the Bible, and living a life that has the Bible at its core. It's an unwavering belief that the Bible is the absolute and only truth, the inspired and inerrant written Word of God that will last forever. The meaning of God's Word doesn't change because society decides they don't like what it says. It's clearly understanding that through Jesus "all things were created: things in heaven and on earth, visible and invisible, whether thrones or powers or rulers or authorities; all things were created by him and for him" (Col. 1:16). It's striving to be transformed to the image of our Creator. It's living our lives to glorify God.

It's subsequently always desiring to do what the Bible says.

Do not merely listen to the word, and so deceive yourselves. Do what it says. Anyone who listens to the word but does not do what it says is like a man who looks at his face in a mirror and, after looking

at himself, goes away and immediately forgets what
he looks like.

—James 1:22–24

The Word is supposed to be as familiar to us as our
own face. This doesn't mean we have to have the entire
Bible memorized, but we need to recognize that God's
Word provides every answer that we will ever need, and
we should be very familiar with it.

Having a biblical worldview is having the same
attitude of Jesus Himself. It's designating Jesus as the
boss of your life,[1] humbling yourself, and submitting
even when we don't feel like it. Jesus Himself prayed on
the Mount of Olives just before His betrayal by Judas
Iscariot: "Father, if you are willing, take this cup from
me; yet not my will, but yours be done" (Luke 22:42).
Even Jesus laid it all down to do the will of His Father.
Follow His lead. Augustine wrote, "God works in us so
that we can have the will to obey. Once we have this
will, God works with us to perfect us." If you haven't
been following Jesus, recommit right now to laying it
all down for Him. It's never too late.

Following Jesus is the most joyful existence you
could ever hope for because it's the full and satisfying
life Jesus promised us: "The thief comes only in order
to steal and kill and destroy. I came that they may have
and enjoy life, and have it in abundance (to the full, till
it overflows)" (John 10:10, AMP).

What is this abundant life? Knowing and loving
God, becoming like Jesus Christ, and making Him
known. It's realizing that we are free to serve God in the

power of the Holy Spirit. Plus, we know our ultimate destiny or as Paul Harvey used to say, "the rest of the story"! Jesus made us this promise: "In my Father's house are many rooms; if it were not so, I would have told you. I am going there to prepare a place for you. And if I go and prepare a place for you, I will come back and take you to be with me that you also may be where I am" (John 14:2–3).

Thank You, Lord Jesus, for this indescribable and irrevocable gift!

We are instructed to walk completely by faith,[2] not by sense knowledge (seeing, hearing, touching, smelling, tasting); even if it doesn't feel right, even if the world ridicules you. The world may call you "old school," out of touch, intolerant, bigoted, evil, narrow minded, a radical right wing conservative, or Jesus freak, just to name a few. But Jesus said, "Blessed are you when people insult you, persecute you and falsely say all kinds of evil against you because of me" (Matt. 5:11). Every second is worth it as you get to know and serve the King of kings!

Biblical or Secular Worldview?

Which worldview do you have? It's easy to find out. Just ask yourself this question: Where is your relationship with Jesus Christ on your list of priorities? He should, of course, be the clear #1 all of the time. How do you know if Jesus is first in your life? To whom or what are you obedient? Who or what is the object of your faith?

According to the Billy Graham Evangelistic Association, about 90 percent of Christians lead defeated lives! They are virtually indistinguishable from the world—lukewarm, too immature or unengaged or lazy or apathetic in their faith. How many Christians know Luke 11:13? We are told, "If you then, though you are evil, know how to give good gifts to your children, how much more will your Father in heaven give the Holy Spirit to those who ask him!" How can we ask God to fill us with His Spirit unless we are willing to empty ourselves through surrender and obedience by knowing and living by what His Word says? Look what the Holy Spirit gives us: "For God did not give us a spirit of timidity (of cowardice, of craven and cringing and fawning fear), but [He has given us a spirit] of power and of love and of calm and well-balanced mind and discipline and self-control" (2 Tim. 1:7, AMP).

Who doesn't want that kind of power in his life? God's children are expected to know His promises (or know where and how to find them) so we can have the strength, boldness, and confidence to represent Jesus Christ to a dying world. All of His promises are in the Bible. "The words and promises of the Lord are pure words, like silver refined in an earthen furnace, purified seven times over" (Ps. 12:6, AMP).

Being filled with the Spirit produces fruit.[3] Producing fruit brings indescribable joy, as Jesus, Paul and Peter point out numerous times in the New Testament, and as I have seen in my life and in numerous other disciples I know. I don't know about you, but I want to be able to stand (in my case I'll be on my knees with my face on the ground) before the Lord Jesus[4] having lived a Spirit-led, fruit-filled life. What about you?

Ignored Love Letters

Imagine that someone very dear to you is away from you for an extended period of time. This person writes you love letters every day, pouring out his heart to you and describing in great detail his love, commitment, promises, and how much you mean to him. Now imagine letting these letters pile up in the closet of a spare bedroom, never once reading them. You may occasionally think about them or even glance at the envelopes every now and then, but you just don't want to sit down and thoroughly enjoy them.

Sound bizarre? Would anyone ever do this? Of course not, that would be ridiculous. Wouldn't everyone want to pore over every word multiple times, basking in the glow of that kind of unconditional love as the writer bares his soul to you? Yet this is how way too many Christians treat their Bibles—God's love letters to you and me. The only way to come to know someone is if that person reveals himself to you. The Bible is the written Word of God revealing Himself to us. He pours out His heart and tangibly demonstrates His unfailing, unconditional love. Sadly, many think that the Bible is some kind of rulebook, a list of do's and dont's, or that it is outdated. These people clearly never read a Bible. Many are "too busy." Many don't really care. Their Bibles are rarely read, possibly looked at occasionally, maybe brought to church, but not likely. However, God says, "Study this Book of Instruction continually. Meditate on it day and night so you will be sure to obey everything written in it. Only then will you prosper and succeed in all you do" (Josh. 1:8, AMP).

Do you want a prosperous and successful spiritual life? There isn't a trial, circumstance, situation, or problem that isn't addressed in the Bible. The Bible equips us to know God and make Him known. It will show us what a morally pure (blameless) and holy life looks like. It will convict us when we go astray and tell us what to do. It is very clear that all of us have meaning in God's eyes because He created us to love us, and He bought us with the blood of His Son. The Bible tells us what he did to demonstrate His love,[5] and how He longs for us to love Him in return.

The Word is so important because:

- It is God's own Word that equips us for everything we do.[6]
- It demonstrates God's unfailing and enduring love and tells us about His fulfilled and future promises (dozens of Scriptures).
- It shows us the way to salvation (eternal life).[7]
- It's the solid foundation of wisdom for life's trials.[8]
- It ushers in our faith.[9]
- It lights our path so we know which way to go.[10]
- It is living and active; a two-edged sword that comforts and guides, convicts, teaches, corrects, and exposes.[11]
- It will do what God intends for it to do.[12]
- We are expected to live by it and do what it says.[13]
- It is the offensive weapon to battle the enemy.[14]

- It can be hidden in our heart so we don't knowingly sin against God.[15]
- And many, many more!

Imagine: God has shared with us the greatest story ever told—the birth, life, death, and resurrection of Jesus Christ—and we won't even bother to read and understand it.

God's Inerrant Word

Jesus is the living Word[16]; the Bible is God's inerrant (free from error or untruth) written Word. "Every word of God is flawless; he is a shield to those who take refuge in him. Do not add to his words, or he will rebuke you and prove you a liar" (Prov. 30:5–6). Please refer to my testimony letter in chapter 1 for a refresher on some specific Bible facts.

We have to be prepared to represent God the Father and God the Savior and God the Teacher, Comforter and Advocate to a skeptical, cynical, and lost world. We have to know Him in order to represent Him. The only way to really get to know Him is to learn about Him from the Bible. God shows us His nature and clearly demonstrates His love, mercy, grace, compassion, patience, plans, heartaches, and will—everything we need to know now about Him while we are here on earth.

A Firm Foundation, an Absolute Truth

We all know that life presents us with significant rewards and challenges. We human beings (both believers and unbelievers) tend to focus on the challenges, what we perceive as the negative. It's human nature. We know, however, that God has given Christians a new nature. This new nature yearns for God and for the real truth. The old nature rebelled against God.

Which nature controls who we are? The one we feed and nurture the most. "Those who are dominated by the sinful nature think about sinful things, but those who are controlled by the Holy Spirit think about things that please the Spirit" (Rom. 8:5 NLT).

The Truth is a person, Jesus Christ.[17] He became flesh and lived among us in order "to seek and to save what was lost" (Luke 19:10).

> Pilate said to Him, Then You are a King? Jesus answered, You say it! [You speak correctly!] For I am a King. [Certainly I am a King!] This is why I was born, and for this I have come into the world, to bear witness to the Truth. Everyone who is of the Truth [who is a friend of the Truth, who belongs to the Truth] hears and listens to My voice.
> —John 18:37–38, AMP

Jesus alone is the Living Word of God, the absolute Truth in a world that pretends there are no absolute truths anymore. The truth is that God chose to look beyond our sin and hopelessness. By His grace, He mercifully gave us a Savior to reconcile Himself to us, a rebellious and obstinate people. He told us all about His plan for our redemption (deliverance from His wrath by the payment of a debt). It's important to live by God's Word in order to pass on the message of reconciliation to a world that is literally going to hell.[18] What other viable option for a Christian is there? "For we speak as messengers approved by God to be entrusted with the Good News. Our purpose is to please God, not people. He alone examines the motives of our hearts" (1 Thess. 2:4, NLT).

Amazingly and sadly, many Christians have never read the Bible from cover to cover, nor do they read it on a regular basis. Consequently, they don't have any idea about how to apply God's precious and powerful Word to their daily lives, which is why, as we learned earlier, that 90 percent live defeated lives. Jesus said,

> Anyone who listens to my teaching and follows it is wise, like a person who builds a house on solid rock. Though the rain comes in torrents and the floodwaters rise and the winds beat against that house, it won't collapse because it is built on bedrock. But anyone who hears my teaching and doesn't obey it is foolish, like a person who builds a house on sand. When the rains and floods come and the winds beat against that house, it will collapse with a mighty crash.
>
> —Matthew 7:24–27, NLT

I started reading the Bible every day in September of 2002. I can't tell you how many hundreds of times I have seen God's transforming work in my life and in the lives of others, all in accordance with the Bible. His word is living and active as any devoted disciple of Jesus Christ can arrest. God equips us so that we can walk with Him in victory: "…thanks be to God! He gives us the victory through our Lord Jesus Christ" (1 Cor. 15:57).

Discipleship

The word *Christian* appears only once in the majority of English Bible translations (Acts 11:26). The words *disciple* or *disciples*, however, appear well over 250 times. In Christianity, a major problem today is that many churches don't require and teach discipleship, but they do encourage membership. Active membership in the body of Christ, using God-given spiritual gifts to strengthen the church, is biblical.[19] Being a member of a reclusive club is not. Some churches perpetuate the notion that there is such a thing as a part-time Christian. As long as you "join their church," come on Sundays, hopefully tithe, and possibly volunteer, everyone is happy.

So many Christians are Christians in name only because they are not making progress toward being true disciples. They are not even being told that they need to! Want proof? Look at the moral morass the United States and Europe are in. Sadly, many Christians think that not being of the world means they shouldn't vote or engage political leadership on issues of morality. That is total deception, a lie from the pit of hell! As Jesus was sent into the world, He sends us into the world: "Just as You [Father] sent Me into the world, I also have sent them into the world" (John 17:18, AMP). He set us apart (sanctified us)[20] for the work we need to do, to deliver the glorious message of salvation, not to congregate in holy huddles or church social clubs that avoid engaging with "those heathens."

Where would we be if Jesus had done this?

Many think that we should just love everyone without addressing sin areas in their lives, especially other Christians who are knowingly sinning. This is completely preposterous and not biblical, either! Jesus never ignored the sin in others' lives—or ours. He cared so much that He came into the world to die on a cross for the sins of *all* mankind.

The apostle Paul exhorted us to "speak the truth in love" (Eph. 4:15), and not to be self-righteous and condemning:

> BRETHREN, IF any person is overtaken in misconduct or sin of any sort, you who are spiritual [who are responsive to and controlled by the Spirit] should set him right and restore and reinstate him, without any sense of superiority and with all gentleness, keeping an attentive eye on yourself, lest you should be tempted also.
>
> —Galatians 6:1, AMP

Do you see why we are commanded to live by every Word that comes from the mouth of God? Talk about a rich and fruitful spiritual life! What do you need to change in your life in order to grow spiritually?

God's Will

I believe that well over 90 percent of God's will for us is in the Bible. For example:

- "Even as [in His love] He chose us [actually picked us out for Himself as His own] in Christ before the foundation of the world, that we should be holy (consecrated and set apart for Him) and blameless in His sight, even above reproach, before Him in love" (Eph. 1:4, AMP).

- "But seek first his kingdom and his righteousness, and all these things will be given to you as well. Therefore do not worry about tomorrow, for tomorrow will worry about itself. Each day has enough trouble of its own" (Matt. 6:33-34).

- "Be joyful always; pray continually; give thanks in all circumstances, for this is God's will for you in Christ Jesus. Do not put out the Spirit's fire; do not treat prophecies with contempt" (1 Thess. 5:16–20).

- "It is God's will that you should be sanctified: that you should avoid sexual immorality" (1 Thess. 4:3).

- "Therefore do not be foolish, but understand what the Lord's will is. Do not get drunk on wine, which leads to debauchery. Instead, be filled with the Spirit" (Eph. 5:17–18).

- "For it is God's will and intention that by doing right [your good and honest lives] should silence (muzzle, gag) the ignorant charges and ill-informed criticisms of foolish persons" (1 Peter 2:15, AMP).

- "How do you know what your life will be like tomorrow? Your life is like the morning fog—it's here a little while, then it's gone. What you ought to say is, 'If the Lord wants us to, we will live and do this or that.' Otherwise you are boasting about your own plans, and all such boasting is evil" (James 4:14–16, NLT).

- Jesus said: "For I have come down from heaven not to do my will but to do the will of him who

> sent me. And this is the will of him who sent me, that I shall lose none of all that he has given me, but raise them up at the last day. For my Father's will is that everyone who looks to the Son and believes in him shall have eternal life, and I will raise him up at the last day" (John 6:38–40).

There are dozens and dozens of Scriptures that tell us His will, because He wants us to have and enjoy the abundant life Jesus died to give us. The rest of His will becomes clearer day-by-day as we willingly submit our will to Christ by obeying the Scriptures. Doing so transforms our minds—we begin to think like Jesus thinks.

We are often too focused on short-term results: Should I date or marry this person, should I take this job, should I buy this house? In one of God's many promises He says: "I will instruct you and teach you in the way you should go; I will counsel you and watch over you" (Ps. 32:8). The question we all should be asking is, "What does God want?" and then be patient and quiet before Him as we wait for the answer. "Be still in the presence of the LORD, and wait patiently for him to act" (Ps. 37:7a, NLT).

All of life's trials, problems, and issues are answered in the Bible. Think of the Bible as the owner's manual for your life. Does it get any better than that?

Under Construction

The apostle Paul wrote in Romans 12:1-2 that if we let Him, God will begin to transform us from the inside out. We may look pretty much the same (though hopefully the joy of salvation will begin to be seen on your facial expressions and in your actions), but we won't act the same. It is important to understand you are now under construction, a work in progress. Oftentimes I wish I had a sign around my neck that said, "Please be patient and understanding with me, I'm being remodeled."

We will not be perfected until we are in the presence of Jesus Himself. Paul summed it up when he said,

> And I am convinced and sure of this very thing, that He Who began a good work in you will continue until the day of Jesus Christ [right up to the time of His return], developing [that good work] and perfecting and bringing it to full completion in you.
>
> —Philippians 1:6, AMP

We are on the narrow path, a lifelong journey of being transformed into the image of Jesus Christ.

What an honor and blessing it is to be on this astonishing journey. When we grow in our knowledge of God and Who He is, we experience indescribable elation and joy, along with trials and suffering, as we are being molded and shaped into the person Jesus envisioned on His journey to the Cross. As we draw closer to God, we begin to see how truly broken we are; how much we need Jesus; and how incredibly loving, faithful, and forgiving our God is. We begin to willingly humble ourselves before Him. I wouldn't trade a moment of this journey for anything the world has to offer! Hallelujah! What about you?

As I reflect on my spiritual growth over the years, I believe two things began to significantly change me. First, I began to listen to God's voice. I started to intentionally pay attention to the Holy Spirit working in and leading me. I sensed early on that He was convicting me (raising my awareness) of a multitude of sins and transgressions, while urging me on to victory over them through Jesus.

It wasn't some mystical audible voice that I heard, or a mediation experience; it came primarily through the Holy Spirit via my pastor, the Bible (by far, the most direction I get is through the Bible), Christian books, and other believers. God always gets my attention when He wants me to learn something. Jesus said, "My sheep listen to my voice; I know them, and they follow me" (John 10:27). I learned that when the Holy Spirit directs me, He leads me firmly in love, always in the small doses He knows I can handle, and always in complete alignment with the Bible.

Are you ready to let the Holy Spirit lead you? Just ask: "Teach me to do your will, for you are my God. May your gracious Spirit lead me forward on a firm footing" (Ps. 143:10, NLT).

At the retreat I mentioned in chapter 2, I was given the book *The Man in the Mirror—The 24 Problems Men Face* by Patrick Morley. Aside from the Bible, this book has had the most impact on my walk with God. I began reading the book every day. I remember asking God to show me areas in my life that needed to be dealt with. I woke up the next morning and opened the book.

The very first thing Morley addressed was the issue of pride. It was as if someone had hit me in the stomach. Pride ruled a lot of things in my life. God was showing me, in no uncertain terms, that pride was a huge problem in my life. "The proud and haughty man—Scoffer is his name—deals and acts with overbearing pride" (Ps. 21:24, AMP).

The second thing that really changed me was that I began to read the Bible every day. Verses came alive.[21] The Word is a two-edged sword; it is powerful. It penetrates to the depths of our innermost being; it transforms us from the inside out as it exposes us for who we really are.[22] It frees us from spiritual bondage and opens our eyes to the awesome God who loves us unconditionally. It is the weapon all believers need to fight off temptation with the truth, and it guides us from ignorance to understanding. Are you ready to start reading the Bible every day? Start today! (See chapter 9.)

Seek His Righteousness First

It takes obedience, discipline, and unwavering faith in God's promises to develop a biblical worldview—living by every word that comes from the mouth of God. None of us can literally live by every Word of God in our frail bodies in this fallen world, but we can follow what Jesus said in Matthew's Gospel:

But if God so clothes the grass of the field, which today is alive and green and tomorrow is tossed into the furnace, will He not much more surely clothe you, O you of little faith? Therefore do not worry and be anxious, saying, What are we going to have to eat? or, What are we going to have to drink? or, What are we going to have to wear? For the Gentiles (heathen) wish for and crave and diligently seek all these things, and your heavenly Father knows well that you need them all. But seek (aim at and strive after) first of all His kingdom and His righteousness (His way of doing and being right), and then all these things taken together will be given you besides. So do not worry or be anxious about tomorrow, for tomorrow will have worries and anxieties of its own. Sufficient for each day is its own trouble.

—Matthew 6:30–34, AMP

We are called to seek God's kingdom and righteousness first, before anything else. Seeking His kingdom first and foremost means allowing Jesus to be the Lord and King of our lives. Seeking righteousness means turning to God first in everything, seeking to please Him, and serving and obeying Him.

How can we possibly do this? We of course look to the Bible: "He renews my strength; He guides me along right paths, bringing honor to his name" (Ps. 23:3, NLT). Jesus, via the Holy Spirit, will lead us—if we are willing to be led. We should be willing to be led by faith alone, *not* by feelings.[23]

Faith is a verb. It isn't something you get. It's something you do. It means *acting* on what you believe. It's a willingness to obey the Master's voice. "So faith comes by hearing [what is told], and what is heard comes by the preaching [of the message that came from the lips] of Christ (the Messiah Himself)" (Rom. 10:17, AMP).

God's Purpose for Us

God reconciled (restored peace, harmony, and fellowship) with us through Christ's death "to present you holy in his sight, without blemish and free from accusation—*if you continue in your faith*, established and firm, not moved from the hope held out in the gospel" (Col. 1:22–23, emphasis mine).

Because Christians have a higher calling[24] it is imperative that we know who we are in Christ and God's purpose for us. In Rick Warren's book *The Purpose Driven Life,* he captured our purposes while we are on this planet:

1. We were planned for God's pleasure—Worship
2. We were formed for God's family—Fellowship
3. We were created to become like Jesus Christ—Discipleship
4. We were shaped to serve God—Ministry
5. We were made for mission—Evangelism

Purpose-driven Christians teach others instead of just being taught. They promote unity, not disunity. They act on their faith instead of being apathetic, doubtful, defeated, and indifferent. They have confidence in God and His many promises instead of living in fear. They evaluate life and circumstances in light of God's Word instead of being driven by feelings, because they know that feelings are oftentimes unreliable.

Purpose-driven Christians also understand that they should either be preparing other believers for acts of service to build up the body of Christ,[25] or that they should be letting themselves be built up. Do you fit into to one of these categories? If not, are you willing to change?

Older but No Wiser

Our world is full of Christians who have aged, but are still infants when it comes to spiritual growth. I believe that is the primary reason the United States, Europe, and other nations are in rapid moral decline.

Millions of Christians have grown older physically without ever maturing spiritually. They act as though spiritual growth is somehow automatic. They may have a plan for retirement, vacations, houses, cars, college expenses, the next job, etc., but they don't have a strategy for enriching their souls and spirits. They leave one of the most important facets of eternal human existence to random chance!

Spiritual growth is not automatic. The author of Hebrews mournfully noted,

> You have been believers so long now that you ought to be teaching others. Instead, you need someone to teach you again the basic things about God's word. You are like babies who need milk and cannot eat

solid food. For someone who lives on milk is still an infant and doesn't know how to do what is right. Solid food is for those who are mature, who through training have the skill to recognize the difference between right and wrong.

—Hebrews 5:12–14, NLT

Immature Christians are spiritual toddlers. Your spirit doesn't grow on its own to maturity any more than a new born baby grows to physical maturity without a lot of care and feeding. You need to have a plan for feeding, nurturing, exercising, and training him. A spirit left on its own withers away, just like our bodies do if they are not properly fed and cared for.

Immature Christians can be new or relatively new believers or believers who have been saved for twenty years, but there was never any appreciable growth. Given the choice of what to eat (if they eat at all), they most likely will head right to sweets, ignoring what is nutritional and has sustenance.

But we all know what happens if you eat only sweets. Our bodies cannot do what they were designed for, and they will become diseased, useless. It's the same thing spiritually. Joy and hope disappear, replaced by despair and anguish as life's inevitable trials and hardships become life's focal points. Before long, the spiritual and emotional euphoria completely evaporates, and we have no idea how to cope with an acute case of spiritual decay. We end up living a defeated life mentioned earlier. We can't know God's nature and love, have hope, or know about His promises without reading and studying the only document that reveals Him.

An example of a "sweet" Scripture is 1 John 3:16a, where the apostle John wrote, "This is how we know what love is: Jesus Christ laid down his life for us." Who doesn't like that? The rest of the verse exhorts and stretches us, however, stating, "And we ought to lay down our lives for our brothers."

Another example of a "sweet" Scripture is, "For God did not appoint us to suffer wrath but to receive salvation through our Lord Jesus Christ" (1 Thess. 5:9). But later on in the chapter Paul writes, "Be joyful *always*; pray continually; Give thanks in *all* circumstances for this is God's will for you in Christ Jesus. Do not put out the Spirit's fire; do not treat prophecies with contempt. Test everything. Hold on to the good. Avoid *every* kind of evil" (1 Thess. 5:16–22, emphasis mine).

How many meals have you missed over the past week? Unless we are dieting, fasting, or working on a deadline and distracted, under unusual stress, or similar circumstances, the answer is usually none; we usually eat multiple times a day because we are hungry and, of course, need the nourishment.

Spiritually mature Christians clearly understand (because they have studied and internalized it) that a daily portion of God's Word is required in order to have a healthy and growing spiritual life. They understand that the only life worth living is the abundant life of knowing God, loving Him, submitting to His will, willing obedience, resisting the devil, drawing near to God (and letting Him draw near to them), and humbling themselves before God because He will lift them up in His perfect timing, according to His perfect plan.[26]

How often do you read and study your Bible? Scripture tells us that the Word will thoroughly equip us for every good work. Yet the Bible is often one of the most under-utilized books a Christian may own. A tremendous amount of Christians never even open it! How can this be?

Maturing in Christ is an act of your will, a commitment you make. When Jesus' disciples decided to follow Him, they didn't understand all of the implications of their decision. They simply expressed a desire to follow Him. That was the beginning of an exciting, life-altering journey!

Are you happy with where you are spiritually? If not, commit right now to change so you can, "Reach unity in the faith and in the knowledge of the Son of God and become mature, attaining to the whole measure of the fullness of Christ" (Eph. 4:13). All growth comes from commitment. Growth requires discipline. Ask the Holy Sprit to help you, and then act on where He leads you. It's the only life worth living. Start today!

It's Our Turn to Forgive

The Bible is very clear that we are completely forgiven in Christ (chapter 1 and 2). Now it's our turn to forgive. When I was thirteen, my mom sat down my brother and me to tell us that our dad was leaving because he didn't love her, he loved someone else. A week later, he was gone. I did a pretty good job of internalizing my anger, resentment, hurt, and rejection. My anger resided just below the surface for decades, manifesting itself occasionally and effectively through my pride.

Twenty-two years after my dad left, I got a phone call from the unlisted operator. (I didn't even know there was such an occupation.) She said there was a Robert Inman who wanted to speak with me. My brother's name is also Robert. I thought maybe he had lost my number. It turned out to be my dad.

A range of mostly unpleasant emotions swept over me during that call, but I accepted his invitation to see him. He seemed genuinely apologetic, so I arranged for both he and my stepmother to visit my family in our home (he lived in another state).

Before he arrived, the thought popped into my mind that he didn't deserve forgiveness. While seriously entertaining this idea, I became pretty agitated. After all, he had missed my graduation from high school and college, my commission and Navy wings ceremonies, my wedding, his grandchildren being born—everything. He had abandoned me. I had a battle raging in my mind.

Just when I had decided not to forgive him, I heard a crystal clear voice in my spirit that simply said, "Who are you not to forgive?"

The Master's Voice

In John 10:27 Jesus said, "My sheep listen to my voice; I know them, and they follow me." I was so far removed from God that I didn't even realize it was Him speaking. But I inherently knew to obey that voice, no questions asked. Right then and there I completely forgave my dad.

He and I had the opportunity to become relatively close over the next few years before he died. One night after a business meeting in Arizona, God gave me the opportunity to hug my dad and tell him that I loved him, something I hadn't done since I was a young boy. What a gracious God, who not only forgave me, He showed me how to forgive Dad. What a precious gift that was!

Why Should We Forgive?

We should forgive those who've hurt us because God forgives us for hurt we've caused Him. Paul states in Colossians 3:13, "Bear with each other and forgive whatever grievances you may have against one another. Forgive as the Lord forgave you."

Forgiving is a command from God, who expects us to forgive unconditionally. He showed us how; just look to the Cross. Forgiving us was an act of God's will. Now it should be an act of our will, regardless if the person deserves it or not, regardless of how we feel. How much did we deserve to be forgiven for the things we have done? You may not feel like you deserve it, but Jesus died on the Cross purchasing (redeeming) us with His blood, demonstrating that we are deserving—period.

We often have a hard time forgiving others because of our pride. I don't know about you, but I have been completely saturated with pride because I was marinating in it for years. Forgiving ourselves and others honors God. Not forgiving honors our pride. In Matthew 6:14–15 Jesus said, "For if you forgive men when they sin against you, your heavenly Father will also forgive you. But if you do not forgive men their sins, your Father will not forgive your sins."

Forgiving should be instantaneous. The ongoing struggle most of us have is dealing with our feelings. Feelings can leave deep scars that take time to heal. I truly believe that if we are sincerely trying and petitioning God to help us handle our feelings, we are honoring His command to forgive. I am so relieved that God knows my true intentions because He knows my heart: "I [the SOVEREIGN LORD] will give you a new heart and put a new spirit in you; I will remove from you your heart of stone and give you a heart of flesh" (Ezek. 36:26). And look what our merciful God does: "God has poured his love into our hearts by the Holy Spirit, whom he has given us" (Rom. 5:5b). When God's love is in your heart, it has to come pouring out to others.

Please, Lord Jesus, empty us of ourselves and fill us with Your love to overflowing. Amen.

Forgive More Than God?

We can never forgive anyone more than God has forgiven us. An attitude of gratefulness results in an attitude of forgiveness. We are completely forgiven in Christ! If you have someone in your life whom you know you need to forgive but haven't, God may be asking you, "Who are you not to forgive?"

Remember, not forgiving honors pride; forgiving honors God. God isn't asking you to forgive anyone more that He has forgiven you. He deserves our complete obedience. Is there anyone you need to forgive and reconcile with? Ask God to help you right now to forgive and forget.

Rights, Privileges, and Responsibilities

As children of God, we have all of the rights, privileges, and responsibilities accorded that position. We love to focus on the rights and privileges, but oftentimes tend to shy away from the responsibilities. Look at what Peter wrote about who we are: "For you are a chosen people. You are royal priests, a holy nation, and God's very own possession. As a result, you can show others the goodness of God, for he called you out of the darkness into his wonderful light" (1 Peter 2:9, NLT).

Priests represent people to God through intercessory prayer, and God to people through tangibly demonstrating the love that God puts in our hearts through the Holy Spirit to others. A teacher of the law asked Jesus what the most important commandment was. Jesus responded, "Love the Lord your God with all your heart and with all your soul and with all your mind and with all your strength. The second is this: Love your neighbor as yourself. There is no commandment greater than these" (Mark 12:30–31). The apostle John added,

> We know that we have come to know him if we obey his commands. The man who says, "I know him," but does not do what he commands is a liar, and the truth is not in him. But if anyone obeys his word, *God's love is truly made complete in him*. This

is how we know we are in him: Whoever claims to
live in him must walk as Jesus did.

—1 John 2:3–6, emphasis mine

Chapter 5

The Second Most Important Prayer

If you don't surrender to Christ, you surrender to chaos. You're free to choose what you surrender to, but you're not free from the consequences of that choice.

—E. Stanley Jones

Obey God and leave the results up to Him. You will *never* regret it.

Now if you will obey me and keep my covenant, you will be my own special treasure from among all the peoples on earth; for all the earth belongs to me.

—Exodus 19:5, NLT

"LORD JESUS, PLEASE take complete control of my life and make me the person You created me to be. Amen."

I firmly believe this is the second most important prayer we will ever pray.

I also believe the second most important prayer is oftentimes more difficult to pray than the most important prayer (chapter 1). When we pray the most important prayer, we receive Christ by faith because the Holy Spirit has testified to our spirit about Christ,[1] convicted us of our guilt in regard to sin,[2] and that reconciliation through Jesus is the only way to salvation.[3] The second most important prayer requires a heartfelt willingness to completely surrender to Jesus Christ. When we have a correct understanding of Jesus Christ, we want to surrender to Him. This is the very heart of worship *and* obedience.

As mentioned in chapter 1, I came out of the pigpen (Luke 15) after thirty years. I was not spiritually or mentally capable or willing to surrender much of anything. God had some serious pruning to do; some long-standing strongholds in me had yet to be dealt with, some of which are still being dismantled.

One of my biggest strongholds was—and still is—pride. It stemmed from being accepted into Aviation Officer Candidate School in the US Navy. My head started to swell, getting bigger and bigger all throughout flight training and getting my wings. Pride became a lifestyle. It defined me. I was always comparing myself to other men, always positioning myself (in my mind) as superior because I flew airplanes. Later on in my business career I used to think that maybe I made more money, had a nicer car and house, and on and on. Ego drove a lot of my thought patterns. But praise God that He made me aware, and changed my heart by giving me the desire to lay it all down. Pride will always be an issue in most of our lives (especially males), but through God's strength it doesn't have to control us.

What or Whom Are You Following?

We love God because He first loved us.[4] We should want to follow Him because as we see His work in our lives and others, we want more: "O taste and see that the Lord [our God] is good! Blessed (happy, fortunate, to be envied) is the man who trusts and takes refuge in Him" (Ps. 34:8, AMP).

God is not a bully or dictator who forces or pesters us into submission. He patiently waits for us to respond.[5] He wants our plans to align with His. He lovingly woos us to Himself, so that we will willingly submit to Him out of an attitude of gratitude. Jesus expects us to follow Him because He paid for our ticket to heaven with His life: "He has given us eternal life, and this life is in his Son. Whoever has the Son has life; whoever does not have God's Son does not have life" (1 John 5:1–12, NLT).

We know that fulfilling His vision for us begins with our obedience. We need to be willing to be shaped into a vessel that God can use: "Yet, O LORD, you are our Father. We are the clay, you are the potter; we are all the work of your hand" (Isa. 64:8). Clay can be both moldable and pliable, or it is dried up, useless to the potter. Jesus modeled perfect obedience for us when He said, "My nourishment comes from doing the will of

God, who sent me, and from finishing his work" (John 4:34, NLT).

We have to know how to be led before we can lead. We have to learn how to be servants before we can do great things for God. We are invited by Jesus to follow Him and are fully expected to accept the invitation. Are you following (or now willing to follow) Him, or are you a Lone Ranger thinking you can still somehow find an abundant, meaningful life without Him?

By following the Holy Spirit's lead,[6] we begin to replace our old nature's character of bitterness, rage, slander, malice, envy, filthy language, evil thoughts, deceit, hatred, greed, self-centeredness, immorality, and more. God's love begins to radiate from us. This kind of love gets people's attention. Jesus Christ becomes real to other people because the Holy Spirit is working through us. Then we become the ambassadors for Jesus Christ that God calls us to be.[7]

Is Jesus Really Your Lord?

Jesus said, "So why do you keep calling me 'Lord, Lord!' when you don't do what I say?" (Luke 6:46, NLT). Paul tells us,

> But each one should be careful how he builds. For no one can lay any foundation other than the one already laid, which is Jesus Christ. If any man builds on this foundation using gold, silver, costly stones, wood, hay or straw, his work will be shown for what it is, because the Day will bring it to light. It will be revealed with fire, and the fire will test the quality

of each man's work. If what he has built survives, he will receive his reward. If it is burned up, he will suffer loss; he himself will be saved, but only as one escaping through the flames.

—1 Corinthians 3:10b–15

Ignoring what Jesus commands and teaches is more foolhardy than building a house with no regard or concern for its foundation, or building a house on the wrong foundation! No one would ever do this, yet way too many of us willfully ignore His commands every day, oblivious or not concerned that we are called to be His disciples (students, followers). Thank You, merciful Father, that You give us multiple chances; You are always faithful to us even though we are not always faithful to You.

The Narrow Path of Surrender

The word *surrender* has extremely negative connotations. Only defeated warriors or criminals surrender or give up. They become captives or slaves to a stronger enemy or face a jail sentence. We don't want to give up anything; we want more! We are conditioned to have it our way, to want and get it now, to be our own man or woman.

Even most Christians aren't willing to completely surrender because of misunderstanding, fear, ignorance, deception, and the perceived loss of control and of what surrendering to Jesus Christ really means. We are deceived into thinking we are holding on to something of value, when in reality it is the spiritual bondage of an unrepentant life that we think we can't live without.

Jesus said, "'I am the vine; you are the branches. If a man remains in me and I in him, he will bear much fruit; apart from me you can do nothing'" (John 15:5). Surrendering to Jesus Christ brings true and lasting freedom.[8]

Tragically, many Christians are living the life of the wrong kind of surrender. It is not the surrender that brings true freedom, but surrender that makes them a captive of the enemy. Disillusioned, frustrated, ill-equipped, misled, with wrong assumptions and a worldview about what being a Christian is all about, they laid down (or never actually put on) the full armor of God.[9]

This armor is the only way to be strong in the Lord and His all-encompassing power. Instead, many chose to remain friends of the world. They want to fit in, be popular and liked by all, never learning that God gives us all we need to fight the good fight of faith, to run the race set out for us, by indwelling us with His own Spirit to handle any and all circumstances as He grows us into the likeness of His Son.

Jesus has completely purchased our freedom by surrendering to the will of His Father[10] so we can have fruitful and productive lives because of who God is, not because of who we are. This is a tough concept for most of us to accept. God-centered people live to please and glorify God. Self-centered people live to glorify themselves. Frank Sinatra's popular song *My Way* epitomized this mindset when he sang, "I did it my way."

Jesus painted an entirely different picture. He said, "If anyone would come after me, he must deny himself and take up his cross daily and follow me" (Luke 9:23). Jesus makes it perfectly clear that He wants us to do it His way, not our way. Why? Because He is the Way, the Truth, and the Life; the only way to heaven. The Creator always knows more, and what's best for the creation. In Psalm 23, David writes that the Lord "guides me in paths of righteousness for his name's sake" (Ps. 23:3b). A joyful, fruitful, and purposeful life is found as we walk along these well-worn and well-marked trails.

God-centered people are willing to walk the narrow and difficult path as they keep their eyes on the prize: "I press on toward the goal to win the [supreme and heavenly] prize to which God in Christ Jesus is calling us upward" (Phil. 3:14, AMP). The prize is spending eternity with Jesus. What could possibly be better than this?

Trust, Then Obey

We inherently know we should trust God much more than we typically do, but it can be scary and unsettling at best.

Fear of the unknown is a huge hurdle to surrendering. Other obstacles to surrendering may include:

- believing God exists, knowing about Him but not knowing Him
- not knowing how God sees you
- not knowing who you are in Christ
- not understanding His divine nature

- harboring pride that fuels an innate desire to be the god of our own lives (loving ourselves more than anything)
- misunderstanding what surrender truly means
- a lack of trust

Your first few baby steps toward surrender are usually met with untold fear, anxiety, doubt, and uncertainty. What am I getting myself into? Will God really take care of me? Is He serious when He says, "Never will I forsake you" (Heb. 13:5)? What proof is there? Do I really want to do this?

As previously mentioned, we are not meant to understand everything about God; we are meant to trust Him. We need to trust in God's promises, because trust is a prerequisite for surrender. We can't trust Him until we know Him well enough to surrender to Him. Why would people depend on someone they don't really trust? We know we can trust God because of how He has always fulfilled His promises. The New Testament is the fulfillment of Old Testament promises: "For all of God's promises have been fulfilled in Christ with a resounding 'Yes!' And through Christ, our 'Amen' (which means "Yes") ascends to God for his glory" (2 Cor. 1:20, NLT).

Surrender and obedience are not based on blind faith. The irrefutable historical proof is there for all to see: God *always* delivers on His promises. He has always proven Himself completely trustworthy. Solomon wrote most of the book of Proverbs to impart wisdom for godly living. He wrote, "Trust in the LORD with all your heart and lean not on your own understanding; in all your ways acknowledge him, and he will make your paths straight" (Prov. 3:5–6).

The more you realize how much God loves you and what He has done for you, the easier surrender becomes. Jesus proved His unconditional love for us and modeled obedience to His Father at the Cross.[11]

True obedience means doing what we are commanded, when we are commanded. I was getting ready to go to Bible study early one Saturday morning. I suddenly got a very strong urge to take some money with me as I rarely carry more than a few dollars. I ignored it, thinking that I could get some at the store later. There was an announcement at the end of Bible study that one of our pastors had a family emergency out of state, and they immediately took up a collection as he was leaving the next day.

I had ignored the urging of the Holy Spirit and missed out on an opportunity. The good news is that I was able to put some money in an offering envelope for him when he got back. Don't forget that God gives us second, third, fourth, and more chances. What is the Holy Spirit urging you to do?

All followers of Jesus Christ come to a crossroad. Either we give Him free rein throughout our entire lives or we leave Him standing by the door with virtually no ability to change our lives.[12] Either we give God permission to transform us to the people He wants us to be or we don't. There is no middle ground. Are you ready to trust God? Ask Him right now to help you in your unbelief and with your doubts.[13]

Being lukewarm—on fire for Jesus one minute and ignoring Him the next—just doesn't work. I lived like this for about two years. Talk about a life of frustration! We can't do anything well—our chosen profession, personal relationships, school, sports, or play an instrument—if we aren't totally committed because we can't be satisfied: The Holy Spirit won't let us. Do you want to be totally committed to God? The Scripture says, "No man who believes in Him [who adheres to, relies on, and trusts in Him] will [ever] be put to shame or be disappointed" (Rom. 10:11, AMP).

I'm learning to trust God more and more by asking Him what He wants me to do in handling life's circumstances such as moving, career, big-ticket purchases, how to handle particular situations, and conversations. I walk in the direction that I think is appropriate and keep asking God if this is what He wants me to do. I try to be sure it isn't something I'm trying to get Him to let me do. If it's a conversation, I ask the Holy Spirit for wisdom or discernment. If it's a difficult situation, I ask for wisdom,[14] and the ability to make sound judgments, and then walk in faith that what I say or do is what He wants me to do. It's absolutely amazing how often God will remove obstacles, put them in the way, guide conversations, provide wisdom, etc. As a wise Christian friend once told me, "The Holy Spirit will meet you right where you are." I love what the Psalmist wrote, "Be still in the presence of the LORD, and wait patiently for him to act" (Ps. 37:7, NLT).

The Best Plan

I was looking at several career options at one time while I was still employed. I felt that I needed to make a change. I applied for dozens of positions for which I was qualified on paper. I had several interviews (second and third interviews and reference checks for some of the positions). But every single time I would pray to God, "Please don't let me have this position if it's not what You want me to do." I never got a single offer over the course of five years! God had another, much better plan; God used me to witness to more than three hundred people in the seven years I was at that company. Then I was offered and accepted an early retirement package that gave me the ability to spend some precious time away with my wife, to finish this book, to be involved in additional ministries, and to purse other career options. Our God is an awesome God!

> Now to him who is able to do immeasurably more than all we ask or imagine, according to his power that is at work within us, to him be glory in the church and in Christ Jesus throughout all generations, for ever and ever! Amen.
>
> —Ephesians 3:20–21

Are You Ready?

As we saw in chapter 3, the growth and maturation process is a component of sanctification. The Holy Spirit convicts us of our desperate need of salvation, but relinquishing control usually comes later. Learning to live in and by the power of the Holy Spirit starts with an attitude of humility (realizing how much we need God), then surrender (wanting to do everything His way).

It took me awhile to realize that we will not experience true freedom unless Jesus is our only boss. Scripture is very clear when it says we cannot serve two masters. We will love the one and hate the other.[15] Jesus said, "If you hold to my teaching, you are really my disciples. Then you will know the truth, and the truth will set you free" (John 8:31–32). He sets us free from being a slave to worry, guilt, shame, anger, resentment, mistrust, and on and on. Free because you are at peace with God; you have His love in your heart; His joy in your life; His passion, purpose, self-control; and the other fruit of the Spirit.[16] Isn't this what you have been yearning for?

A friend of mine had a serious alcohol problem. His life revolved around the cocktail hour. He was beginning to come back to the Lord after a three-decade absence as God was making His presence known in his life. He was invited to go to a Christian retreat with his daughter. He really didn't want to go, but decided at the last minute that he would do it for her.

Very early one morning he found himself in the chapel. There was a book where several people had laid down their sins (what they were in bondage to) at the feet of Jesus with written statements asking Him to take control. And that is just what he did. He asked the Lord Jesus to help him stop drinking. He hasn't had a drink since! Don't ever forget that we serve an awesome God, with Whom "all things are possible" (Mark 10:27).

What strongholds are holding you captive? What sins are holding you in bondage? Are you ready to lay them down at the feet of Jesus right now? Look at what Paul wrote:

> But he [God] said to me, "My grace is sufficient for you, for my power is made perfect in weakness." Therefore I will boast all the more gladly about my weaknesses, so that Christ's power may rest on me. That is why, for Christ's sake, I delight in weaknesses, in insults, in hardships, in persecutions, in difficulties. For when I am weak, then I am strong.
>
> —2 Corinthians 12:9–10

Attitude Check

For most of us, it is natural to be somewhat independent (either because we're trained that way or we've had to do so as a means of survival). Our parents prepare us (or eventually show us the door) to be on our own and live our own lives.

We usually learn the world's way of doing most everything, because the vast majority of what we are exposed to is from a secular worldview, not a biblical perspective. We are under an illusion that we have control of our lives. Most of the time things seem to go our way, feeding the fire of the deception. I remember a popular fast food chain's advertising slogan of "Have it your way." Another advertiser coined the slogan "I want it all and I want it now."

James, a half-brother of Jesus, summed it up well when he wrote,

> Now listen, you who say, "Today or tomorrow we will go to this or that city, spend a year there, carry

on business and make money." Why, you do not even know what will happen tomorrow. What is your life? You are a mist that appears for a little while and then vanishes.

—James 4:13–14

Does anyone know what will happen tomorrow? What about five minutes from now? I have learned that one of the few things that I really have control over in life is my attitude. What we believe determines how we behave. Having an attitude of gratitude toward God because of what He has done, is doing, and will do will completely transform your life. A heart of gratitude and thankfulness is a heart that wants to serve God.

James also wrote, "Now someone may argue, 'Some people have faith; others have good deeds.' But I say, 'How can you show me your faith if you don't have good deeds? I will show you my faith by my good deeds'" (James 2:18, NLT).

What is the state of your heart? How's your attitude? The Bible is the great attitude-adjuster.

Let Go and Let God

It is very difficult letting go of what we hold dear, especially if we have held it for long periods of time. I used to hold a lot of things as very dear: money, job titles, prestige, cars, competitiveness, and pride, to name a few. The more God revealed Himself to me, the less and less I wanted to hold on tightly to the things that have no eternal value. I began to hunger and thirst for more of God in my life as the Holy Spirit began to teach me things like love, joy, peace, patience, kindness, and other fruit of the Spirit,[16] along with mercy, grace, trust, obedience, and forgiveness.

Jesus promised that the Holy Spirit will "guide us into all truth" (John 16:13). This means we have to let ourselves be led. Being led requires us to make a choice and then act on it. Remember, faith is acting on what you believe. Are you ready to confess that Jesus is the Boss of your life and give Him control?

In Philippians chapter 3, the apostle Paul talks about how he had every reason to have confidence in his own efforts as he was a Pharisee who obeyed the law without fault. He goes on to say,

> I once thought these things were valuable, but now I consider them worthless because of what Christ has done. Yes, everything else is worthless when compared with the infinite value of knowing Christ Jesus my Lord. For his sake I have discarded everything else, counting it all as garbage, so that I could gain Christ and become one with him. I no longer count on my own righteousness through obeying the law; rather, I become righteous through faith in Christ. For God's way of making us right with himself depends on faith.
>
> —Philippians 3:7–9, NLT

Paul says that he wants to experience everything about Jesus. Talk about an attitude of surrender! How badly do you want to experience Jesus?

God Pleasers

It's so easy to love ourselves and do what pleases us. That described me perfectly for a big part of my life (and still does in certain areas). The Bible, however, teaches us to submit, follow, be humble and deny ourselves, serve, and be obedient. That's why it's called the narrow road, because it's is the most difficult way. But the rewards are well worth it: "Behold, I am coming soon! My reward is with me, and I will give to everyone according to what he has done" (Rev. 22:12).

In Philippians chapter 2, Paul describes how Jesus modeled the behavior He expects from us by humbling Himself and becoming obedient to death, even to the worst way of dying, being crucified on a cross. But then we see that His Father exalted Him to the highest place, and gave Him a name that is above every name because of His submission to His Father's will (verse 9). We believers are told to humble ourselves and God will exalt us.[17] Humility is realizing that since God is our Creator, Father, Lord, Savior, Redeemer, Comforter, Advocate, Counselor, and Teacher, our existence and righteousness depend entirely on Him.

Ask your heavenly Father right now to empty you of you and fill you with His Spirit: "If you then, though you are evil, know how to give good gifts to your children, how much more will your Father in heaven give the Holy Spirit to those who ask him!" (Luke 11:13).

Now God can really start to work in your life.

Be Used by God

Everything we need, God has! He doesn't invite (call) the qualified for His use; He qualifies everyone He invites. We are all invited. Look at what the author of Hebrews prayed:

> Now may the God of peace—who brought up from the dead our Lord Jesus, the great Shepherd of the sheep, and ratified an eternal covenant with his blood—may he equip you with all you need for doing his will. May he produce in you, through the power of Jesus Christ, every good thing that is pleasing to him. All glory to him forever and ever! Amen.
>
> —Hebrews 13:20–21, NLT

The big question is whether or not we will accept the invitation. God always provides plenty of opportunities. He is looking for those who are contrite (sincerely remorseful of past sins) in spirit: "This is the one I esteem: he who is humble and contrite in spirit, and trembles at my word" (Isa. 66:2b). The Bible is replete with broken people whom God invited to represent Him—murderers, prostitutes, liars, thieves, adulterers, hypocrites, and on and on. These were people just like you and me. Paul wrote in 2 Corinthians chapter 4 that we are "jars of clay" (imperfect, broken, flawed vessels) that possess a precious treasure, the light of the divine Gospel, and that the power of the Gospel is from God. His majesty and glory are on display and made perfect through human weakness. God uses our own weaknesses and brokenness to demonstrate His strength. What a calling! What blessing!

Are you excited about your weaknesses? Are you ready right now to let God use them for His glory?

Bill Bright founded Campus Crusade for Christ on the UCLA campus in 1951. In 1965, he wrote what he called "the distilled essence of the gospel" into a booklet called *Have You Heard of the Four Spiritual Laws?* Bright wanted to produce a movie about the life of Jesus Christ. He worked with Hollywood producer John Heyman to make the film *Jesus* (also called *The Jesus Film*), which is based on the Gospel of Luke. This movie has been seen by several billion people since 1979. It is estimated that more than two hundred million people have received Jesus Christ as their Lord and Savior by viewing it.

When asked why God has used and blessed his life so much, Bright replied, "When I was a young man I made a contract with God. I literally wrote it out and signed my name at the bottom. It said, 'From this day forward, I am a slave of Jesus Christ.'"

I have made this commitment in writing to Jesus Christ as well. Will you?

We have already seen that we are saved by God's grace, and that we receive this free gift through faith in Jesus Christ. We should also know by now that works are a result of our attitude of gratitude toward God for what He has done, is doing, and will do for us, and that works are *not* the means to salvation. Works are the result of salvation. We should be willing to let God use us for His glory. He will use us if we make ourselves available. All we have to do is ask. He will work through the new creation that you have become to show the world that He is real, alive, and actively engaged, longing to reconcile everyone to Himself through Jesus Christ.

Has God ever used you? Have you ever grieved over the lost, resulting in your witnessing to a friend, relative, or stranger; walked alongside someone who was going through a tough time; randomly helped someone in need; helped at a food drive or shelter; prayed with fervor for someone; or done a random act of kindness with no expectation of something in return? Did you ever volunteer because you really wanted to, not because you felt you had to (legalism) or because you wanted recognition (pride)?

Remember the joy you felt? Not happiness, which is a temporary and transient emotion, but pure joy because you were acting on the power and desire God had given you to do what pleases Him. We are designed by God to experience this joy! No one can take away this joy, nor can any circumstance. Has your joy diminished?

Joy comes when you are fulfilling the purpose for which God created you, and remembering how much He has done, is doing, and will do for you.

> All praise to God, the Father of our Lord Jesus Christ. It is by his great mercy that we have been born again, because God raised Jesus Christ from the dead. Now we live with great expectation, and we have a priceless inheritance—an inheritance that is kept in heaven for you, pure and undefiled, beyond the reach of change and decay. And through your faith, God is protecting you by his power until you receive this salvation, which is ready to be revealed

on the last day for all to see. So be truly glad. There is wonderful joy ahead, even though you have to endure many trials for a little while. These trials will show that your faith is genuine. It is being tested as fire tests and purifies gold—though your faith is far more precious than mere gold. So when your faith remains strong through many trials, it will bring you much praise and glory and honor on the day when Jesus Christ is revealed to the whole world. You love him even though you have never seen him. Though you do not see him now, you trust him; and you rejoice with a glorious, inexpressible joy. The reward for trusting him will be the salvation of your souls.

—1 Peter 1:3–9, NLT

What a phenomenal passage! God is so good! Ask God right now to help you restore your joy; He will!

Because God has set you apart, your changed attitude of love, devotion, obedience, and joy will show that He is real to an unbelieving, cynical world. This is what it means to be an ambassador for Jesus Christ. The prophet Isaiah responded to God's request of "Whom shall I send?" by responding, "Here am I, send me!" (Isa. 6:8). James exhorted us to "Submit yourselves, then, to God. Resist the devil, and he will flee from you. Come near to God and he will come near to you…Humble yourselves before the Lord, and he will lift you up" (James 4:7–8, 10).

We Have God's Vision of Us to Fulfill

It takes time, study, and a willingness to know God to realize that He is the only answer to everything in life.

We are born with a spiritual emptiness in our lives that only He can fill (because of the fall of Adam).

Everyone tries to fill this emptiness with something. Everything we try to combat emptiness with (except God) will eventually destroy us, some sooner than others—drugs, alcohol, money, power, possessions, success, control, astrology, sex, greed, religious activities, and on and on. But nothing will ever come close to satisfying; even though most people will look everywhere else for satisfaction and fulfillment, except to God. We can all run from God, but we can never hide: "The eyes of the LORD are everywhere, keeping watch on the wicked and the good" (Prov. 15:3).

We will all give an account of our lives to Jesus Christ; we will stand before him on our own: "For we must all appear before the judgment seat of Christ, that each one may receive what is due him for the things done while in the body, whether good or bad" (2 Cor. 5:10). Five minutes from now you could be dead. Are you ready to stand before Jesus? Are you absolutely confident He will say, "Well done, my good and faithful servant"?

God wants all of us, not just the leftovers or our attention only when we are in crisis. He wants to be involved in every detail of our lives. "The Lord directs the steps of the godly. He delights in every detail of their lives" (Ps. 37:23, NLT). Ninety-nine percent is not enough. An airline captain flying you from Los Angeles to Boston doesn't say, "Welcome aboard. I have good news. We are going to get you 99 percent of the way to Logan airport today."

Our lives don't turn out like we planned because God is so good. Hebrews 12:2 tells us Jesus "for the joy set before Him endured the shame of the cross." I believe the joy set before Jesus was completing the work His Father had given Him, and a clear vision of the person you could be if He died as your substitute. We bring joy to God when we truly try to live a surrendered, obedient life. Remember, Jesus surrendered everything for you and me. Everything. Are you ready to give everything to Him?

> You are the light of the world. A city set on a hill cannot be hidden. Nor do men light a lamp and put it under a peck measure, but on a lampstand, and it gives light to all in the house. Let your light so shine before men that they may see your moral excellence and your praiseworthy, noble, and good deeds and recognize and honor and praise and glorify your Father Who is in heaven.
>
> —Matthew 5:14–16, AMP

Chapter 6

Glorification

God will never be a debtor to anyone. That means that any "sacrifice" we make or hardship we endure for His sake and by His Spirit, He will amply reward out of all proportion to what we suffered.[1]

For [the Spirit which] you have now received [is] not a spirit of slavery to put you once more in bondage to fear, but you have received the Spirit of adoption [the Spirit producing sonship] in [the bliss of] which we cry, Abba (Father)! Father! The Spirit Himself [thus] testifies together with our own spirit, [assuring us] that we are children of God. And if we are [His] children, then we are [His] heirs also: heirs of God and fellow heirs with Christ [sharing His inheritance with Him]; only we must share His suffering if we are to share His glory.

—Romans 8:15–17, AMP

Future Salvation

GLORIFICATION IS FUTURE tense, God's final phase of salvation. It is the completed renovation of our body, soul, and spirit into Christ's magnificent splendor where we will be saved from the presence of sin for eternity because we will be in the very presence of our Lord Jesus Christ:

> Now the dwelling of God is with men, and he will live with them. They will be his people, and God himself will be with them and be their God. He will wipe every tear from their eyes. There will be no more death or mourning or crying or pain, for the old order of things has passed away.
> —Revelation 21:3–4

Hallelujah!

God's Glory, Not Our Glory

There are so many things to love and enjoy about God. One of my favorites is that He knows my heart so much better than I do. He knows that I want to glorify and please Him in everything, even when my actions fall short. And He continues to love and pursue me even when I fall short or run the other way, as Jonah did (Jonah 1). He is God the Teacher, Comforter, and Advocate (the Holy Spirit), my assurance that I haven't been orphaned by God.[2]

When was the last time you said Thank You to the Holy Spirit for His ministry in you?

When God looks at us, He sees us as we really are: "the LORD searches every heart and understands every motive behind the thoughts" (2 Chron. 28:9). He also sees us as to who we will be: "God who gives life to the dead and calls things that are not as though they were" (Rom. 4:17); then calls us to fulfill His vision. We are all a work in progress as God patiently molds us into the image of Jesus.

Glory is an attribute of God's character that emphasizes His greatness, power, majesty, and authority. God uses us for His glory when we praise His name and obey His commandments. We see God's divine glory through Christ in the New Testament: "The Word became flesh and made his dwelling among us. We have seen his glory, the glory of the One and Only, who came from the Father, full of grace and truth" (John 1:14).

Divine glory is not seeking glory for us, just as Christ did not seek glory for Himself. He always sought to bring glory to His Father: "Jesus replied, 'If I glorify myself, my glory means nothing. My Father, whom you claim as your God, is the one who glorifies me'" (John 8:54). We believers should always seek to worship, praise, and honor the Lord Jesus.

Sharing Jesus' Glory

God will glorify His children: "Because of our faith, Christ has brought us into this place of undeserved privilege where we now stand, and we confidently and joyfully look forward to sharing God's glory" (Rom. 5:2, NLT).

God's children will share in the glory of Jesus Christ. I don't know what this means exactly. I can't even begin to imagine how incredibly spectacular, wonderful, and rewarding that will be. But it will be beyond fantastic, way beyond anything our physical senses can currently handle.

What is the best day or days you have ever had? Looking back on my life, there were several notable days. The day I came to a saving faith in Jesus Christ, the day I rededicated my life to the Lord. The day I was married. The days my children were born. But the best by far is yet to come! One second in God's presence will far surpass anything we have ever experienced. The very best day I ever enjoyed on this earth won't begin to compare to sharing in Christ's glory.

Do you see why we should have continual joy with thanksgiving in our hearts regardless of our circumstances? Christians should be the most joyful people on the planet by far, because we know how the story of our life on this earth will end! That is why we worship Him and give Him all praise honor and glory; it's practice and preparation for when we will be dwelling in God's physical presence. Thank You, Lord Jesus, my magnificent Savior!

Take notice! I tell you a mystery (a secret truth, an event decreed by the hidden purpose or counsel of God). We shall not all fall asleep [in death], but we shall all be changed (transformed). In a moment, in the twinkling of an eye, at the [sound of the] last trumpet call. For a trumpet will sound, and the dead [in Christ] will be raised imperishable (free and immune from decay), and we shall be changed (transformed). For this perishable [part of us] must put on the imperishable [nature], and this mortal [part of us, this nature that is capable of dying] must put on immortality (freedom from death).

—1 Corinthians 15:51–53, AMP

We Will Get a Glorified Body

I can't wait! I will no longer have back problems, cavities, aching knees, a need for glasses, hair loss, or any other ailment. We will be completely free from sin and suffering, as we see in Revelation chapter 21. With our new bodies, we will be able to be in the very physical presence of God forever. Our physical body (or the remains of our physically dead body) will be transformed in the twinkling of an eye (in probably something like a billionth of a second) into a body that will never decay.

Scripture gives us a few glimpses of what it will be like to be in the presence of God. In Revelation 4:1–6 (AMP) the apostle John wrote about an astonishing scene that was shown to him by God:

AFTER THIS I looked, and behold, a door standing open in heaven! And the first voice which I had heard addressing me like [the calling of] a war trumpet said, Come up here, and I will show you what must take place in the future. At once I came under the [Holy] Spirit's power, and behold, a throne stood in heaven, with One seated on the throne! And He Who sat there appeared like [the crystalline brightness of] jasper and [the fiery] sardius, and encircling the throne there was a halo that looked like [a rainbow of] emerald. Twenty-four other thrones surrounded the throne, and seated on these thrones were twenty-four elders (the members of the heavenly Sanhedrin), arrayed in white clothing, with crowns of gold upon their heads. Out from the throne came flashes of lightning and rumblings and peals of thunder, and in front of the throne seven blazing torches burned, which are the seven Spirits of God [the sevenfold Holy Spirit]; And in front of the throne there was also what looked like a transparent glassy sea, as if of crystal.

Can you even begin to imagine being in such a place? It will be absolutely incredible!

John goes on to write that the twenty-four elders and four "living creatures" give glory, honor and thanks to God day after day and night after night (v. 10). Everyone in heaven will bask in God's magnificent splendor for eternity.

That is why we will need a new, perfect body. We will exchange our perishable bodies with imperishable ones. We will trade mortality with immortality. Only this perfect, glorified body[3] will be able to handle His love; enjoy the sights, sounds, and worship; and be in His presence 24/7.

I can't wait to be face to face with Jesus forever, but I realize He has work for us to do before we get there.[4] But what a blessing it is to know the rest of the story!

It doesn't get any better than this! Can you see why Christians should strive daily to please, honor, represent, and glorify God?

Make Time Today for God

I always want to be prepared for Christ's Second Coming. I want to know God as much as I possibly can right now. I want to experience Him in every aspect of my life. How about you?

I inherently knew the way to do this was to spend quiet time with Him, but as it turned out I needed direct encouragement on how and what to do. My mentor (if you don't have a mature Christian mentor of the same gender, pray that God will provide one for you as He did for me) summed it up in my first visit with him. He told me that I had head knowledge about God, but I needed more heart knowledge.

I needed to spend quiet time with God every day and just be still before Him.[5] This is in addition to Bible reading and presenting your prayers and petitions.[6] Morning personally works for me, but the key is to do it every day at pretty much the same time. After a week or so it becomes not only a habit, but something you really look forward to.

This is no talking, petitioning, or expectation; I'm just hanging out with my heavenly Father. He gets the first part of my day, every day, because He deserves it. I used to think I had to sit quietly and wait for God to show up. The Holy Spirit taught me that my heavenly Father is already waiting for me every morning!

There have been times when I have felt a spiritual connection that I can't describe other than to say it is intensely wonderful. Many days I don't seem to have any connection at all, but in His Word He promises me He is there: "The LORD your God is with you, he is mighty to save. He will take great delight in you, he will quiet you with his love, he will rejoice over you with singing" (Zeph. 3:17).

Other times I have had peaceful serenity and calmness as I quietly worship Him in spirit. This is not because I am super-spiritual, but because I take the time to be with my Creator with a heart of worship and gratitude: "Come near to God and he will come near to you" (James 4:8a)!

Are you ready to experience His love, peace, and rest? Start spending quiet time before God today. You will *never* regret it!

A Foretaste of Divine Glory

Spending time with God, experiencing His unfailing love and rest, is perfect preparation for being in heaven. God gives His devoted followers sneak peeks of heaven every now and then if we are paying attention, since "we have the Holy Spirit within us as a foretaste of future glory" (Rom. 8:23, NLT). This foretaste makes us hunger and thirst for more.

Don't strive to be comfortable here on earth. Our citizenship is in heaven.[7] A Christian's life on earth is preparation for heaven, our ultimate destination. Strive to be more and more like Jesus every day. Each day that allows us to do so is a gift from the Father of heavenly lights.[8]

> I have fought the good (worthy, honorable, and noble) fight, I have finished the race, I have kept (firmly held) the faith. [As to what remains]

henceforth there is laid up for me the [victor's] crown of righteousness [for being right with God and doing right], which the Lord, the righteous Judge, will award to me and recompense me on that [great] day—and not to me only, but also to all those who have loved and yearned for and welcomed His appearing (His return).

—2 Timothy 4:7–8, AMP

Chapter 7

Lessons Learned

Biblical wisdom unites God, the Source of all understanding, with daily life, where the principles of right living are put into practice.

—Jack Hayford

For wherever there is jealousy (envy) and contention (rivalry and selfish ambition), there will also be confusion (unrest, disharmony, rebellion) and all sorts of evil and vile practices. But the wisdom from above is first of all pure (undefiled); then it is peace-loving, courteous (considerate, gentle). [It is willing to] yield to reason, full of compassion and good fruits; it is wholehearted and straightforward, impartial and unfeigned (free from doubts, wavering, and insincerity).

—James 3:16–17, AMP

Wisdom from Above

ORGANIZED RAW DATA becomes information. Information applied becomes knowledge. The Bible tells us that fear of the LORD (worshipping Him with reverence and awe) is the beginning of knowledge.[1] Knowledge appropriately applied becomes wisdom as the Holy Spirit will lead us into all truth.[2] Heavenly wisdom comes from God alone:

> My child, listen to what I say, and treasure my commands. Tune your ears to wisdom, and concentrate on understanding. Cry out for insight, and ask for understanding. Search for them as you would for silver; seek them like hidden treasures. Then you will understand what it means to fear the LORD, and you will gain knowledge of God. For the LORD grants wisdom! From his mouth come knowledge and understanding.
>
> —Proverbs 2:1-6, NLT

Be committed to obtaining knowledge, ask God for wisdom, then act on it once you receive it.[3] Ask Him right now!

Model Jesus Christ

Jesus Christ is in complete control. Paul tells is in Colossians 1:17, "He [Jesus] is before all things, and in him all things hold together" (brackets added). Whether we embrace and enjoy this reality or not is totally up to us. Either we learn from Him or we will wallow in spiritual ignorance. I have decades of experience to prove it.

The more we know Jesus, the more irresistible He is, and the more we want to be like Him. I am coming to know more and more about Jesus through Scripture, being around other believers, and seeing the Holy Spirit's transforming work in my life and in the lives of others. Aside from His creation and His Word, God is the most real in my life because of the significant changes I have seen in myself and other believers.

As we become more like Jesus, we inherit His servant's heart.[4] For example, I actively place Bible tracts most everywhere I go. I share my testimony letter or verbal testimony whenever I can. I wake up every morning and ask God what is on His agenda for me that day. I tell Him that I am completely dependent on Him. I pray Psalm 139:23-24 frequently: "Search me, O God, and know my heart; test me and know my anxious thoughts. See if there is any offensive way in me, and lead me in the way everlasting."

I pray that I am filled to overflowing with the Holy Spirit[5] all of the time, so that I may bring honor and glory to God in what I do, think, and say.

God's fingerprints are everywhere in our lives if we will only take the time to look and listen. If you aren't seeing them, ask the Holy Spirit to open up your spiritual eyes and then take the time to listen and observe. God never forces Himself on us. He tenderly and always lovingly chips away at the veneer of deceit and lies that keep us from a deeper relationship with Him. This veneer keeps us in love with ourselves, the world, and sin with its empty promises and disastrous results (as we should know quite well by now).

Praise God that He sees beyond the train wreck our lives are, that His will is to use us for His purposes:

> In a large house there are articles not only of gold and silver, but also of wood and clay; some are for noble purposes and some for ignoble. If a man cleanses himself from the latter, he will be an instrument for noble purposes, made holy, useful to the Master and prepared to do any good work.
>
> —2 Timothy 2:20–21

Because your beliefs directly determine your behavior—you will be recognized (positively or negatively) by your fruit (works, actions, attitude). Unconditional, selfless love always turns heads as evidenced by Jesus' life. Do what pleases God by setting yourself aside for the Master's use.

Lessons Learned

Since coming back to the Lord Jesus, I've learned or am learning that:

- Being a dedicated and disciplined disciple (student and follower) of Jesus Christ is the only way to become like Him.
- Reading the Bible every day and doing what it says will positively and dramatically transform your life (pray for understanding before you begin to read).

- It's not how we start the race; it's how we finish it. Commit to God and to yourself right now that you will finish strong.
- Christians are forgiven sinners, saints who sin.
- We need to live like we're forgiven—not feeling guilty, ashamed, defeated, or inadequate because we were bought and paid for with the blood of Jesus Christ.
- Jesus' death on the cross means that we are forgiven for every sin we have committed and will ever commit.
- Jesus' death on the cross freed me from the power of sin—my heart's desire is to live a life that pleases Him.
- We'll never forgive anyone more than God has forgiven us.
- We're one of many poster children of God's amazing grace, forgiveness, tender mercy, and unconditional love.
- Christians belong completely to God. Everything we need, He has. Our next breath, heartbeat, smile, sunrise, sunset, trial—everything—is a gift from Him.
- Pride will ensnare us; humbling ourselves before God frees us.
- Anger and bitterness will destroy us.
- We are supposed to tell people about Jesus Christ.
- The Holy Spirit instills a constant hunger and thirst in us to know God, and to make Him known.

- The more I know Jesus, the more I hunger and thirst for more of Him.
- Failure is never final, unless we let it be.
- Life's trials will purify our faith if we let them.
- God changes lives, performs miracles, and answers prayer. Nothing is impossible for Him.
- Obedience unlocks God's power in and through us.
- No one cares what we know or what we think or what we do until they know we care.
- God calls us to be witnesses, not lawyers or judges.
- We get what we confess with our mouths.
- We have to tenaciously guard what we're feeding our minds:
  - TV, news, newspapers, movies, radio, Internet
  - Whom we spend time with
- We will grow in whatever we commit to.
- We don't change the gospel message; the gospel message changes us.
- Faith requires action. Faith is acting on what we believe.
- We can't give away what we don't have.
- Love, not nails, kept Jesus on the cross.
- Being sick and tired of being sick and tired is a terrible way to live.
- Being lukewarm or lackadaisical for God is a miserable way to live.

- The closer we get to God, the closer He comes to us.
- The closer we get to God, the more broken we realize we are and the more we realize we need to depend completely on Him.
- We need to ask God to reveal Himself to us.
- In life or in death, we belong to God.
- One person with God is a majority.
- Our real identity is in Christ—confident, secure, humble, strong, victorious, and loving.
- God always keeps His promises; we can put our hope in them.
- It's not what we have, but what we allow God to do in and through us that results in significance.
- Do not let what you don't know to interfere with what you do know.
- God doesn't call the qualified; He qualifies the called.
- The only thing faster than light is darkness retreating from the light.
- Worry is taking on a burden God never intended us to have.
- Coincidence is when God chooses to remain anonymous.
- It's not the outcome, it's the process.
- We should always do the right thing because it honors and pleases God.
- God promises a safe landing, not a calm passage.
- We will never get tired of Jesus in our lives.

- God is in the process of changing us; we are a work in progress.
- God tests us, not to grade us, but to grow us to be more like Jesus.
- Evolution is true science fiction.
- The Big Bang theory is true: God spoke and BANG! it happened.
- Only what is done for Jesus Christ will last.
- We shouldn't base our joy on outward circumstances.
- We should pray from our heart: "Lord Jesus, please take complete control of my life and make me the person You created me to be. Amen."
- We should join a small group in our churches (be sure to pray about it).
- We should participate in a Bible study group and put into practice what we learn.
- Fellowship is essential as a disciple of Jesus Christ (pray about this).
- The tasks ahead of us are never as great as The Power behind us.
- We should read a daily devotional and/or read it to our families.
- We should intercede for the lost in prayer—write their names on a piece of paper if we need to—pray for them frequently for as long as it takes.
- We should pray that God will give us the boldness to share the gospel.
- I'm positive that if I die tonight I'm going to heaven to be with Jesus Christ. Are you?

- We should put together a list of the Scriptures that impacts us the most and keep them in our Bibles and refer to them frequently.
- Memorizing Scripture is important to our growth, as the Word is an essential weapon in God's armament. Not knowing any Scripture is tantamount to going to a sword fight without a sword.
- We all are ministers (not pastors). We need to use our God-given talent to serve God and people.
- We weren't put here to like the world; we were put here to change it by being devoted followers and ambassadors of Jesus Christ.
- It is God's job to solve the problems of the world. Our job is to walk in humble obedience and do what God wants us to do.

All has been heard; the end of the matter is: Fear God [revere and worship Him, knowing that He is] and keep His commandments, for this is the whole of man [the full, original purpose of his creation, the object of God's providence, the root of character, the foundation of all happiness, the adjustment to all inharmonious circumstances and conditions under the sun] and the whole [duty] for every man. For God shall bring every work into judgment, with every secret thing, whether it is good or evil.

—Ecclesiastes 12:13, AMP

Chapter 8

What Do I Do Now?

No one is useless to God, no one.

—Max Lucado

So we make it our goal to please him, whether we are at home in the body or away from it. For we must all appear before the judgment seat of Christ, that each one may receive what is due him for the things done while in the body, whether good or bad.

—2 Corinthians 5:9–10

God's Plan

GOD'S OVERALL PLAN is made clear in Scripture:

God has now revealed to us his mysterious plan regarding Christ, a plan to fulfill his own good pleasure. And this is the plan: At the right time he will bring everything together under the authority of Christ—everything in heaven and on earth. Furthermore, because we are united with Christ, we have received an inheritance from God, for he chose us in advance, and he makes everything work out according to his plan.

—Ephesians 1:9–11, NLT

Furthermore,

Both Gentiles and Jews who believe the Good News share equally in the riches inherited by God's children. Both are part of the same body, and both enjoy the promise of blessings because they belong to Christ Jesus…. *God's purpose in all this was to use the church to display his wisdom in its rich variety to all the unseen rulers and authorities in the heavenly places.* This was his eternal plan, which he carried out through Christ Jesus our Lord.

—Ephesians 3:6, 11, NLT, emphasis mine

God's individual plan is for His children to be conformed into the spiritual likeness of His Son.[1]

What Is <u>the</u> Goal for Your Life?

I don't know about you, but my life's goal is to be an active and willing participant in God's plans. I want everyone to see that Jesus is real because of my life. My goal is to be as much like Jesus as I can possibly be, always striving to please and glorify Him as His fully devoted disciple. Effectively focusing my energy on this goal will directly determine what kind of husband, father, brother, son, uncle, friend, subordinate, co-worker, elder, speaker, or author that I am and will be.

Needless to say, it can be tough, frustrating, discouraging, and challenging, and oftentimes I fall short. King David wrote, "If the LORD delights in a man's way, he makes his steps firm; though he stumble, he will not fall, for the LORD upholds him with his hand" (Ps. 37:23–24). Thank You, Father!

I am living each day to be able to someday hear the words of the Master: "Well done, you upright (honorable, admirable) and faithful servant! You have been faithful and trustworthy over a little; I will put you in charge of much. Enter into and share the joy (the delight, the blessedness) which your master enjoys" (Matt. 25:23, AMP).

What is your life's goal, the one thing that you must complete or continuously strive for before you pass away? Does it need to change to align with what God wants?

Respond to Your High Calling as a Royal Priest

God's grace does not negate our duty to obey. We were not called to live a comfortable, insulated life and to congregate only in holy huddles to avoid any contact with "those heathens." We are called into a ministry of reconciliation as ambassadors of Jesus Christ.[2]

God equips us with His very own armor "so that you can take your stand against the devil's schemes" (Eph. 6:11). There is no higher calling in the universe than being "a chosen people, a royal priesthood, a holy nation, a people belonging to God, that you may declare the praises of him who called you out of darkness into his wonderful light" (1 Peter 2:9).

Belonging to a royal priesthood means through direct communication you are to be bringing people to God through prayer and intercession, and bringing God (representing Him) to people with love, by witnessing, actions, and deeds (see chapter 4, on our purposes in life). God expects our willing participation in His sovereign plan. We will be judged on what we do with what He gave us at the judgment seat of Christ. This is nothing to be frightened about; just ask God to show you how to be the person He created to be. God wants to help us to fulfill our purpose on this planet, not keep us guessing and in fear of what we may be doing wrong.

I ask God what I can do for Him each day, and He always shows me. Some days it can be as simple as His showing me the most beautiful sunset I have ever seen to remind me of His eternal power. I respond by thanking Him profusely for giving me the ability to see and enjoy His glory. Other days I may have the opportunity to tell someone about Jesus, or to minister to someone who is hurting, or to spend time with my spouse or children with whom God has richly blessed me. Remember, our purpose is to glorify God, and we definitely do when we appreciate the things He does for us.

I completely trust that He will give me the wisdom, discernment, judgment, insight, skills, and strength to do whatever He asks of me. As I mentioned earlier, it is very important to understand that God doesn't call the qualified, He qualifies whom He calls. What is He calling you to do? Will you accept His invitation?

Respond to God's Faithfulness

Praise God that He is always faithful, even when we aren't. The story of the lost (prodigal) son is an amazing example of God's mercy, forgiveness, and unconditional love. As I mentioned, I was one of these as I had drifted away from God for thirty years. I got caught up in thinking that the pleasures of the world were the highest good. Life was ultimately all about me and my wants.

To me, the most amazing part about the lost son story is that the Father (God) *ran* to His son as soon as He saw him: "But while he was still a long way off, his father saw him and was filled with compassion for him; he ran to his son, threw his arms around him and kissed him" (Luke 15:20). If we stray (and regardless of how long), the Lord waits patiently for us to turn back to Him, even if we have disgraced Him. And when we do, He runs to us with open arms, rejoicing at our return. That's phenomenal!

You Are Blessed When Insulted

I was in a bookstore once when I noticed a young man (probably early high school age) looking at books in the New Age section. I walked up and handed him a Bible tract and told him that Jesus, not New Age literature, has all of the answers, that He alone is our salvation. As I was leaving the store, I heard a woman's voice behind me yelling, "You pervert!" I turned around in time to have the boy's mother shove the crumpled Bible tract at me and call me a pervert again.

Initially I was taken aback until I remembered that Jesus encourages us in these circumstances: "Blessed are you when people insult you, persecute you and falsely say all kinds of evil against you because of me. Rejoice and be glad, because great is your reward in heaven, for in the same way they persecuted the prophets who were before you" (Matt. 5:11–12). I have prayed (interceded) for that woman and her son on many occasions that they would come to a saving faith in Jesus.

God gave us the Holy Spirit to give us the strength and boldness for any situation when we need it. He blesses us so that we can be a blessing to others. How awesome is that?

Be Disciplined

It takes purpose, discipline, and focus to accomplish any goal. Anyone who has been in athletics, dancing, debate, public speaking, acting, or music, or has pursued a college degree or vocation, etc., knows that the only way to get better at something is to discipline ourselves to do whatever it takes. Most of us are pretty disciplined already. How many of us always take the time to watch out favorite TV show or sporting event? How about visiting our favorite coffee shop, restaurant, retail stores, checking e-mail or catching up on social websites? We are disciplined to do the things we really want to do. All of us have been given the ability to discipline ourselves spiritually as well with the Holy Spirit's help. But most of us choose not to discipline ourselves in the things of God. Jesus is looking for dedicated and disciplined students with a desire to learn:

To the Jews who had believed him, Jesus said, "If you hold to my teaching, you are really my disciples. Then you will know the truth, and the truth will set you free." They answered him, "We are Abraham's descendants and have never been slaves of anyone. How can you say that we shall be set free?" Jesus replied, "I tell you the truth, everyone who sins is a slave to sin. Now a slave has no permanent place in the family, but a son belongs to it forever. So if the Son sets you free, you will be free indeed."

—John 8:31-36

I love and thank God for this freedom! What a precious gift. This freedom comes from knowing who we are in Christ. We know who we are in Christ because God has revealed Himself to us in His Word. There is no substitute for God's Word. (See Recommended Resources for some ideas about daily Bible reading.)

Spend quiet time with God and prayer time with Him. In 1 Thessalonians 5:16 we are told to "pray continuously." No one can pray all of the time, but we can have a prayerful attitude, realizing that we are totally dependent on Him for everything (even our next breath). We can talk with Him, thank Him throughout the day, praise Him, ask for wisdom and guidance, share our frustrations and struggles, pray that the person driving by us on the road going twenty miles over the speed limit will come to a saving faith, show us how to be Christ's ambassador to our neighbors and unsaved friends, etc. I am greatly comforted that God always wants to hear from me, and He listens to what I have to say. What an incredible blessing!

Get Engaged in the Battle

We as Christians sometimes find ourselves stressed, struggling, overcommitted, and sometimes overwhelmed. This has led many to be apathetic, marginalized, defeated, angry, outraged, discouraged, disillusioned, and on and on. That's not who we are supposed to be in Christ: "God opposes the proud but favors the humble. So humble yourselves under the mighty power of God, and at the right time he will lift you up in honor. Give all your worries and cares to God, for he cares about you" (1 Peter 5:5–7, NLT).

I take great comfort in this Scripture, realizing that when I get anxious I can ask God to help me so that I may glorify and represent Him instead of focusing on me and my problems.

The spiritual battle raging for our hearts and minds is intense. You may have heard the metaphor about the white and black dog. The white dog is our new nature. It is constantly at war with the black dog (our old nature's conditioned response to life's circumstances). Who will win this battle? The one you feed the most, of course. Which one are you feeding?

Satan's goal is to remove you from the truth of God's Word to render you an ineffective Christian who is both unwilling and unable to lead others to Christ. This is why we must equip ourselves for the battle every day.

Purpose in Your Mind to Finish Well

It's not how you start the race, however; it's how you finish. God equips us with everything we need to finish strong. Scripture encourages us to:

- Submit yourself to God, yield to His will, and ask what He wants you to do—then say yes to whatever it is.[3] Resolve in your mind right now to be obedient, regardless of your circumstances or comfort level.[4]

- Resist the devil (in the power of the Holy Spirit)[3]; stay in the Word, fellowship, Bible study.[5] Stand firm in God's armor.

- Draw near to God, and He will draw near to you.[6]

- Ask God to purify your heart.[7] Lead a morally pure life.[8]

- Grieve and be mournful over your sins. Be humble before God (realize your insignificance and complete dependence on Him) and He will lift you up in honor and use you in ways you can't even imagine![9] Sin demonstrates just how much you need Jesus involved in every detail of your life.[10]

Make Commitments to God

Here are the commitments I have made to God:

- I will do whatever You ask of me, regardless of how difficult it is.
- I will love my wife as Christ loved the church and gave Himself up for her.[11]
- I will be the father to my children the way You are to me.
- I will deny myself, pick up my cross daily, and follow You.

- I will be the spiritual leader You have called
me to be in my family, work, church, and
community.

I have to completely depend on the strength of Jesus
and follow the Holy Spirit's leading if I am to have any
chance of meeting these commitments. As Paul said, "I
thank Christ Jesus our Lord, who has given me strength
to do his work. He considered me trustworthy and
appointed me to serve him" (1 Tim. 1:12, NLT).

I struggle and fail at times, but then I get up and
try again. Failure is never final unless you allow it to
be, and we serve a forgiving God of grace and mercy
who knows our true motives. Fortunately, God is our
Advocate, Comforter, and Encourager, not an indifferent
and distant tyrant to the struggles of His children.

What is God asking you to do? If you don't know,
ask Him. What commitments have you made or are
willing to make right now? Why don't you write a note
to God and sign your name dated today?

Walk by Faith with Unshakeable Hope

Faith is not a feeling. Our faith shouldn't waiver because
we aren't feeling very spiritual today. We now know that
faith requires action. It isn't something we passively
stumble upon; it's something we do. Hope is being
sure what we believe will happen (the return of Jesus
Christ, for example). There is no hope without a solid
foundation of faith.

What or who is the object of your faith? Your faith
is worth no more than what you choose to put it in. My

faith is Jesus Christ and Him alone. My hope is in His promises. Jesus has *never* let me down. He always fulfills His promises: "Let us hold unswervingly to the hope we profess, for he who promised is faithful" (Heb.10:23).

Work Out Your Salvation

In Philippians 2:12–13, Paul offers insight into spiritual growth while speaking to people who already believe: "Continue to work out your salvation with fear and trembling, for it is God who works in you to will and to act according to his good purpose." Certain cults will tell you that this scripture proves that the path to salvation is by works. On the contrary! Notice that it says work *out*—not work *on*—your salvation. There is nothing you can do to save yourself. Christ took care of that by His life, death, and resurrection. The important thing to note is that God has a part in our growth, but so do we. We must make an intentional effort to grow daily because of our love for the God who saved us: "Our God is a God who saves; from the Sovereign LORD comes escape from death" (Ps. 68:20).

The Only Viable Plan

Because God is so good, my life didn't turn out like I had planned, and neither will yours. I had envisioned a life of flying for the airlines and riding around on a Harley, independent and free. God had other plans. Right after I got off of active duty (US Navy), President Reagan fired all the air traffic controllers. Plus I had met this beautiful girl to whom I have now been married for almost three decades and we have two grown children. God used internal turmoil at one of the companies I worked for as a catalyst to get my focus on Him. That's a blessing! God is always so good!

Billy Graham's wife, Ruth, once said that if God had granted her prayers about a husband, she would have married the wrong man several times. Come near to God. Wake up every morning and say, "Good morning, Lord. I'm reporting for duty. What is on Your agenda today? Please show me how I can bear fruit that will last and bring glory to Your name."

Worship

Offering yourself completely to God is what worship is all about. Human beings were created to be worshipers of God; we are to glorify and exalt Him and Him alone. Worship the Creator and not the creation nor what creations we obtain (cars, boats, jewelry, houses): "You shall have no other gods before or besides Me" (Ex. 20:3, AMP). Why would you want any gods besides Him?

Worship (corporate or private) is the human response to the self-revelation of God. Worship consists of praise, thanksgiving, humbling ourselves, acknowledging His goodness with an attitude of reverence and awe, rejoicing in song, reading, studying and meditating on Scripture, being still before Him, using and enjoying the gifts and talents He has given us, and simply enjoying Him and His glorious creation.

Worship glorifies God and brings Him pleasure as we give ourselves completely to Him—all day, every day. Paul wrote: "So whether you eat or drink, or whatever you do, do it all for the glory of God" (1 Cor. 10:31, NLT).

Meticulously Avoid All Idols

An idol is anything in your life that is more important to you than God. You can readily tell if you have idols in your life by looking at where you spend your time and energy. We can get deceived by the culture into thinking that we will not be happy until we have _____.
Here is a partial list of today's idols:

- money
- power
- career
- recognition
- titles and positions
- homes (i.e., attaching personal worth and identity to a dwelling)
- country club memberships (i.e., being part of the "right" crowd, being seen)
- craving ministry titles (e.g., elder, deacon)
- relationships (e.g., idolizing a spouse, boyfriend/ girlfriend)
- movie stars
- sports stars
- famous and wealthy people
- gambling
- food
- clothes
- lust
- greed

- evil desires
- anger
- sex
- pornography
- television
- movies
- video games
- alcohol
- affiliations with "important" people
- cars, boats, planes, motorcycles
- our bodies (i.e., physical appearance)
- "superior" intelligence

Cling to the Solid Rock

God never changes: "Jesus Christ is the same yesterday, today, and forever" (Heb. 13:8). It's how we respond to Him that changes, if we do indeed chose to change. He will never force us into believing or accepting Him as He has given each of us the freedom to choose.

He invites us into a close relationship. He longs to reveal Himself to us and move into our hearts.[12] He longs to have us love Him in return. The apostle Peter wrote, "If anyone speaks, he should do it as one speaking the very words of God. If anyone serves, he should do it with the strength God provides, so that in all things God may be praised through Jesus Christ" (1 Peter 4:11).

I have never regretted serving God.

Be encouraged! It doesn't get any better than this! Jesus said "In the world you have tribulation and trials and distress and frustration; but be of good cheer [take courage; be confident, certain, undaunted]! For I have overcome the world. [I have deprived it of power to harm you and have conquered it for you.]" (John 16:33, AMP). God gives us everything we need to praise, honor and glorify Him. We just need to give Him our heart.

> How great is the love the Father has lavished on us, that we should be called children of God! And that is what we are! The reason the world does not know us is that it did not know him. Dear friends, now we are children of God, and what we will be has not yet been made known. But we know that when he appears, we shall be like him, for we shall see him as he is.
>
> —1 John 3:1–2

Chapter 9

Recommended Resources

Don't focus on the enormity of the work that needs to be done, focus on the value of the harvest. You will *never* regret making an eternal investment in someone.

For God is the one who provides seed for the farmer and then bread to eat. In the same way, he will provide and increase your resources and then produce a great harvest of generosity in you. Yes, you will be enriched in every way so that you can always be generous. And when we take your gifts to those who need them, they will thank God.

—2 Corinthians 9:10–11, NLT

HERE ARE SOME of the resources I have come across that have helped me in my walk with Jesus.

Daily Bible Study

It is easy to see Jesus in the lives of devoted followers of Christ. But the best way to know Him is to study His own Word. I strongly recommend that you develop the habit of reading the Bible *every day*. A daily read Bible is a convenient way to go. In twenty to thirty minutes per day, you can read the entire Bible through in a year. There are several "read the Bible in one year" Bibles available in numerous translations (NIV, KJV, NKJV, NLT, etc.). A particular favorite Bible study guide of mine is *How to Study the Bible for Yourself* by Tim LaHaye. Your church should have a plan for reading the Bible through in a year. And, of course, there is always the Internet. One of my favorite websites is www.Biblegateway.com.

I really like Life Application Study Bibles and Student Bibles. They contain numerous application notes that are very useful in increasing your understanding. In addition, they typically offer dictionaries/concordances, a master index, Bible reading plans, Christian worker resources guides, maps, and more. I believe experts say that if you do the same thing at the same time for three weeks, it becomes a habit. This is one habit you definitely want to have! Read the Bible right after your quiet time and prayer time. Start today!

I need to conscientiously put Jesus in my thoughts all the time. One way to keep Jesus in your thoughts is to spend time in the Word. God will talk to you through the Bible as the Holy Spirit reveals spiritual truths to you. What a beautiful treasure. "I have hidden your word in my heart, that I might not sin against you" (Ps. 119:1).

Web Sites

Bible websites that are my favorites include:
- www.BibleGateway.com
- www.bible.org
- www.bibles.net
- www.biblica.com

News and events websites that I enjoy are:
- www.OneNewsNow.com
- www.afa.net
- www.OneMillionMoms.com
- www.OneMillionDads.com
- www.FocusOnTheFamily.com
- www.SaveCalifornia.com
- www.CoralRidge.org

Here are some excellent evangelism websites:
- www.chick.com
- www.CustomTractSource.com
- www.IAmSecond.com
- www.LivingWaters.com
- www.markcahill.org
- www.WayOfTheMaster.com

Here is my favorite men's ministry website:
- www.ManInTheMirror.org

Here is an excellent women's ministry website:
- www.WomenOfFaith.com

These are great Christian legal rights organizations:
- www.aclj.org
- www.faith-freedom.com
- www.pacificjustice.org

Other meaningful websites include:
- www.christianmovies.com
- www.expelledthemovie.com/videos.php
- www.dayspring.com/ecards
- www.freewebs.com/ratorrey
- www.gospel.com
- www.maninthemirror.org/biblestudy/register.htm
- www.TheSecondMostImportantPrayer.com
- www.worldvision.org

Books

- *100% Guarantee*—Steve Magill
- *30 Life Principles*—Charles Stanley
- *Experiencing God*—Henry Blackaby & Claude King
- *Humility True Greatness*—C. J. Mahaney
- *Kingdoms in Conflict*—Charles Colson
- *Loving God*—Charles Colson
- *My Heart, Christ's Home*—Robert Boyd Munger
- *One Thing You Can't Do in Heaven*—Marc Cahill
- *One Heartbeat Away*—Marc Cahill
- *Pilgrim's Progress*—John Bunyan
- *Prevailing Prayer*—D.L. Moody
- *Secret Power*—D.L. Moody
- *Secrets of the Vine*—Bruce Wilkinson

- *Seven Seasons for the Man in the Mirror*—Patrick Morley
- *The Journey*—Billy Graham
- *The Man in the Mirror*—Patrick Morley
- *The Prayer of Jabez Devotional*—Bruce Wilkinson
- *The Purpose Driven Life*—Rick Warren

What Are You Feeding Your Mind?

- Find a Christian radio station in your area that features solid biblical teaching.
- Get an audio Bible and follow along in your Bible. Then listen to the audio and solely concentrate on the audio with eyes closed. Often I will pray in accordance with the Scriptures as I hear them read.
- Consider subscribing to Sky Angel (www. SkyAngel.com).
- Put an Internet software filter on your computers if you have children or if you are struggling with pornography. You can have an accountability partner install the software and keep the password to himself.
- Use parental controls on cable and satellite TV channels in your home.
- Record spiritual milestones by keeping a spiritual journal. Mine primarily consists of experiences I have during my quiet time with God or significant events. I do not have daily entries. Some people track prayers and how and when they are answered. The important issue is to have one near your Bible and to use it. You

will be amazed as you look back over the years at how much you have grown or learned and/or what God has done in your life and the lives of others around you.

Engage and Positively Influence the Culture—Evangelize

- Download my testimony letter and edit it for your specific testimony (www.TheSecondMostImportantPrayer.com). Share it electronically or in printed form.
- Give impactful Christian movies (*Facing the Giants, The Perfect Stranger, Another Perfect Stranger, Fireproof, Amazing Grace, One Night with the King, The Jesus Movie, Passion of the Christ, Faith Like Potatoes, Mother Teresa, The Heart of Texas* and many more), along with some chocolates to your neighbors, co-workers, friends, and relatives with a card saying how blessed you are to know them, or how blessed you are that they are your neighbor. Or give your testimony letter, or tell what Christmas and Easter is really all about. God put them in your life, whether you like them or not. Be sure to pray about opportunities to witness to them.
- High-quality Bible tracts cost about four to fifteen cents each (one hundred for four to fifteen dollars) at this writing, plus shipping and tax. Put them in your bills and other mail correspondence. Leave them on gas station pumps, in restrooms, at payphones, or in grocery stores. Use your

imagination. For four cents you can lead someone to a saving faith in Jesus Christ! The apostle Paul wrote, "I planted the seed, Apollos watered it, but God made it grow" (1 Cor. 3:6).

- Man in the Mirror Ministries (www. ManInTheMirror.org) has a *Books! by the Box* ministry where you can get cases of books for just over a dollar per book. Books are fantastic witnessing tools.
- Ask people, "If you were to die tonight, are you 100 percent sure you are going to heaven?" Be prepared to tell them what Jesus has done in your life.
- Pray that God will put harvesters into His harvest field (including you); for we are told: "The harvest is plentiful, but the workers are few. Ask the Lord of the harvest, therefore, to send out workers into his harvest field" (Luke 10:2).
- Pray what Paul did when he said,

And pray for me, too. Ask God to give me the right words so I can boldly explain God's mysterious plan that the Good News is for Jews and Gentiles alike. I am in chains now, still preaching this message as God's ambassador. So pray that I will keep on speaking boldly for him, as I should.

—Ephesians 6:19–20, NLT

I Will See You in the New Jerusalem

As we know, salvation is not a one-time event. It is an exhilarating journey that lasts for eternity. We have been wonderfully blessed by God to be a blessing to everyone we encounter.

Because I serve an incredibly awesome and mighty God who has adopted me into His family, I desperately want more of Him in my life. Why? Because I am in awe of Who He is and amazed at how much He loves me. Frankly, it's hard for me to believe how much He loves me at times. I always want to please Him because of what He has done, is doing, and will do for me. He deserves all of my loyalty. He deserves all of me. Subsequently, I have dedicated the rest of my life to serving Him. Are you ready to make that commitment? Make up your mind right now to be a faithful and obedient ambassador for Jesus Christ every day for the rest of your life and pray,

> Lord Jesus, please take complete control of my life and make me the person You created me to be. Amen.

I pray that this book has encouraged you. We don't completely understand why God loves us so much that He gave His only Son so we can know, enjoy, and love Him for eternity. But because He did; let's exalt Him, and praise His name forever. I can't wait to exchange success stories with you about our joyous journeys when I see you in the New Jerusalem, where we will worship The GREAT I AM together for eternity!

> All praise to God, the Father of our Lord Jesus Christ. It is by his great mercy that we have been born again, because God raised Jesus Christ from the

dead. Now we live with great expectation, and we have a priceless inheritance—an inheritance that is kept in heaven for you, pure and undefiled, beyond the reach of change and decay. And through your faith, God is protecting you by his power until you receive this salvation, which is ready to be revealed on the last day for all to see. So be truly glad. There is wonderful joy ahead, even though you have to endure many trials for a little while. These trials will show that your faith is genuine. It is being tested as fire tests and purifies gold—though your faith is far more precious than mere gold. So when your faith remains strong through many trials, it will bring you much praise and glory and honor on the day when Jesus Christ is revealed to the whole world. You love him even though you have never seen him. Though you do not see him now, you trust him; and you rejoice with a glorious, inexpressible joy. The reward for trusting him will be the salvation of your souls.

—1 Peter 1:3–9, NLT

Endnotes

Chapter 1: The Most Important Prayer

1. "For all have sinned and fall short of the glory of God" (Romans 3:23).

2. "For the wages of sin is death, but the gift of God is eternal life in Christ Jesus our Lord" (Romans 6:23).

3. "For even the Son of Man did not come to be served, but to serve, and to give his life as a ransom for many" (Mark 10:45).

4. "God made him who had no sin to be sin for us, so that in him we might become the righteousness of God" (2 Corinthians 5:21).

5. "For God loved the world so much that he gave his one and only Son, so that everyone who believes in him will not perish but have eternal life. God sent his Son into the world not to judge the world, but to save the world through him" (John 3:16-17, NLT).

6. "Therefore, if anyone is in Christ, he is a new creation; the old has gone, the new has come!" (2 Corinthians 5:17).

7. "But we are looking forward to the new heavens and new earth he has promised, a world filled with God's righteousness" (2 Peter 3:13, NLT).

8. "He predestined us to be adopted as his sons through Jesus Christ, in accordance with his pleasure and will" (Ephesians 1:5).

9. "THEREFORE, [there is] now no condemnation (no adjudging guilty of wrong) for those who are in Christ Jesus, who live [and] walk not after the dictates of the flesh, but after the dictates of the Spirit. For the law of the Spirit of life [which is] in Christ Jesus [the law of our new being] has freed me from the law of sin and of death" (Romans 8:1–2, AMP).

10. "The Spirit himself testifies with our spirit that we are God's children. Now if we are children, then we are heirs—heirs of God and co-heirs with Christ, if indeed we share in his sufferings in order that we may also share in his glory" (Romans 8:16–17).

11. "In My Father's house there are many dwelling places (homes). If it were not so, I would have told you; for I am going away to prepare a place for you. And when (if) I go and make ready a place for you, I will come back again and will take you to Myself, that where I am you may be also" (John 14:2–3, AMP).

12. "Jesus replied, I assure you, most solemnly I tell you, before Abraham was born, I AM" (John 8:58, AMP); "If you had known Me [had learned to recognize Me], you would also have known My Father. From now on, you know Him and have seen Him... Jesus replied, Have I

been with all of you for so long a time, and do you not recognize and know Me yet, Philip? Anyone who has seen Me has seen the Father. How can you say then, Show us the Father? …Believe Me that I am in the Father and the Father in Me; or else believe Me for the sake of the [very] works themselves. [If you cannot trust Me, at least let these works that I do in My Father's name convince you.]" (John 14:7, 9, 11, AMP).

13. "But when the teachers of religious law who were Pharisees saw him [Jesus] eating with tax collectors and other sinners, they asked his disciples, 'Why does he eat with such scum?' When Jesus heard this, he told them, 'Healthy people don't need a doctor—sick people do. I have come to call not those who think they are righteous, but those who know they are sinners'" (Mark 2:16–17, NLT).

14. "I have been crucified with Christ and I no longer live, but Christ lives in me. The life I live in the body, I live by faith in the Son of God, who loved me and gave himself for me" (Galatians 2:20).

15. "Therefore everyone who hears these words of mine and puts them into practice is like a wise man who built his house on the rock. The rain came down, the streams rose, and the winds blew and beat against that house; yet it did not fall, because it had its foundation on the rock. But everyone who hears these words of mine and does not put them into practice is like a foolish man who built his house on sand. The rain came down, the streams rose, and the winds blew and beat against that house, and it fell with a great crash" (Matthew 7:24-27).

16. "But anyone who does not love does not know God, for God is love…We know how much God loves us, and we have put our trust in his love. God is love, and all who

live in love live in God, and God lives in them" (1 John 4:8, 16, NLT).

17. "We know what real love is because Jesus gave up his life for us. So we also ought to give up our lives for our brothers and sisters" (1 John 3:16, NLT).

18. The phrase (at the beginning of the chapter) does not appear in the testimony letter available at TheSecondMostImportantPrayer.com. The sample prayer to receive the Lord Jesus is there instead.

Chapter 2: Justification

1. For our sake He made Christ [virtually] to be sin Who knew no sin, so that in and through Him we might become [endued with, viewed as being in, and examples of] the righteousness of God [what we ought to be, approved and acceptable and in right relationship with Him, by His goodness]" (2 Corinthians 5:21, AMP).

2. "Let us draw near to God with a sincere heart in full assurance of faith, having our hearts sprinkled to cleanse us from a guilty conscience and having our bodies washed with pure water" (Hebrews 10:22).

3. "Whoever believes in the Son has eternal life, but whoever rejects the Son will not see life, for God's wrath remains on him" (John 3:36).

4. "THEREFORE, [there is] now no condemnation (no adjudging guilty of wrong) for those who are in Christ Jesus, who live [and] walk not after the dictates of the flesh, but after the dictates of the Spirit. For the law of the Spirit of life [which is] in Christ Jesus [the law of our new being] has freed me from the law of sin and of death" (Romans 8:1–2, AMP).

5. "…Man is not justified by observing the law, but by faith in Jesus Christ. So we, too, have put our faith in Christ Jesus that we may be justified by faith in Christ and not by observing the law, because by observing the law no one will be justified" (Galatians 2:16).

6. "To him [Jesus] who loves us and has freed us from our sins by his blood" (Revelation 1:5c).

7. "I am the true vine, and my Father is the gardener" (John 15:1).

8. "You adulterous people, don't you know that friendship with the world is hatred toward God? Anyone who chooses to be a friend of the world becomes an enemy of God" (James 4:4).

9. "Taste and see that the LORD is good; blessed is the man who takes refuge in him" (Psalm 34:8).

10. "And I am certain that God, who began the good work within you, will continue his work until it is finally finished on the day when Christ Jesus returns" (Philippians 1:6, NLT).

11. "Humble yourselves, therefore, under God's mighty hand, that he may lift you up in due time" (1 Peter 5:6); "Humble yourselves before the Lord, and he will lift you up in honor" (James 4:10, NLT).

12. "So he returned home to his father. And while he was still a long way off, his father saw him coming. Filled with love and compassion, he ran to his son, embraced him, and kissed him… But his father said to the servants, 'Quick! Bring the finest robe in the house and put it on him. Get a ring for his finger and sandals for his feet. And kill the calf we have been fattening. We must celebrate with a feast, for this son of mine was dead and has now

returned to life. He was lost, but now he is found.' So the party began" (Luke 15:20, 22-24, NLT).

13. "He [Jesus] is the one all the prophets testified about, saying that everyone who believes in him will have their sins forgiven through his name" (Acts 10:43, NLT).

14. "Come near to God and he will come near to you. Wash your hands, you sinners, and purify your hearts, you double-minded. Grieve, mourn and wail. Change your laughter to mourning and your joy to gloom" (James 4:8–9).

Chapter 3: Sanctification

1. "The LORD directs the steps of the godly. He delights in every detail of their lives" (Psalm 37:23, NLT).

2. "So if the Son sets you free, you will be free indeed" (John 8:36).

3. "For God is working in you, giving you the desire and the power to do what pleases him" (Philippians 2:13, NLT).

4. "Do not be conformed to this world (this age), [fashioned after and adapted to its external, superficial customs], but be transformed (changed) by the [entire] renewal of your mind [by its new ideals and its new attitude], so that you may prove [for yourselves] what is the good and acceptable and perfect will of God, even the thing which is good and acceptable and perfect [in His sight for you]" (Romans 12:2, AMP).

5. "But when he, the Spirit of truth, comes, he will guide you into all truth. He will not speak on his own; he will speak only what he hears, and he will tell you what is yet to come" (John 16:13); "For if you live according to the

sinful nature, you will die; but if by the Spirit you put to death the misdeeds of the body, you will live, because those who are led by the Spirit of God are sons of God" (Romans 8:13-14).

6. "Don't you realize that all of you together are the temple of God and that the Spirit of God lives in you?" (1 Corinthians 3:16, NLT).

7. "But he said to me, 'My grace is sufficient for you, for my power is made perfect in weakness.' Therefore I will boast all the more gladly about my weaknesses, so that Christ's power may rest on me. That is why, for Christ's sake, I delight in weaknesses, in insults, in hardships, in persecutions, in difficulties. For when I am weak, then I am strong'" (2 Corinthians 12:9–10).

8. "And do not grieve the Holy Spirit of God [do not offend or vex or sadden Him], by Whom you were sealed (marked, branded as God's own, secured) for the day of redemption (of final deliverance through Christ from evil and the consequences of sin)" (Ephesians 4:30, AMP).

9. "Do not quench (suppress or subdue) the [Holy] Spirit" (1 Thessalonians 5:19, AMP).

10. "But you will receive power when the Holy Spirit comes on you; and you will be my witnesses in Jerusalem, and in all Judea and Samaria, and to the ends of the earth" (Acts 1:8).

11. "Dear friends, you always followed my instructions when I was with you. And now that I am away, it is even more important. Work hard to show the results of your salvation, obeying God with deep reverence and fear" (Philippians 2:12, NLT).

12. "Your attitude should be the same as that of Christ Jesus: Who, being in very nature God, did not consider

equality with God something to be grasped, but made himself nothing, taking the very nature of a servant, being made in human likeness. And being found in appearance as a man, he humbled himself and became obedient to death— even death on a cross!" (Philippians 2:5–8).

13. "'I am the Vine; you are the branches. Whoever lives in Me and I in him bears much (abundant) fruit. However, apart from Me [cut off from vital union with Me] you can do nothing'" (John 15:5, AMP).

14. "Do not be anxious about anything, but in everything, by prayer and petition, with thanksgiving, present your requests to God. And the peace of God, which transcends all understanding, will guard your hearts and your minds in Christ Jesus" (Philippians 4:6–7).

15. "Let us fix our eyes on Jesus, the author and perfecter of our faith, who for the joy set before him endured the cross, scorning its shame, and sat down at the right hand of the throne of God" (Hebrews 12:2).

16. "I have been crucified with Christ and I no longer live, but Christ lives in me. The life I live in the body, I live by faith in the Son of God, who loved me and gave himself for me" (Galatians 2:20).

17. "God saved you by his grace when you believed. And you can't take credit for this; it is a gift from God. Salvation is not a reward for the good things we have done, so none of us can boast about it" (Ephesians 2:8–9, NLT).

18. "But someone will say, 'You have faith; I have deeds.' Show me your faith without deeds, and I will show you my faith by what I do... As the body without the spirit is dead, so faith without deeds is dead" (James 2:18, 26).

19. "Let us hold unswervingly to the hope we profess, for he who promised is faithful" (Hebrews 10:23).

20. "Be strong and courageous. Do not be afraid or terrified because of them, for the LORD your God goes with you; he will never leave you nor forsake you" (Deuteronomy 31:6).

21. "...God has poured out his love into our hearts by the Holy Spirit, whom he has given us" (Romans 5:5b).

22. "The next day John saw Jesus coming toward him and said, 'Look, the Lamb of God, who takes away the sin of the world!'" (John 1:29).

23. "But the LORD is the true God; he is the living God, the eternal King" (Jeremiah 10:10a); "We know also that the Son of God has come and has given us understanding, so that we may know him who is true. And we are in him who is true—even in his Son Jesus Christ. He is the true God and eternal life" (1 John 5:20).

Chapter 4: Biblical Worldview

1. "If you confess with your mouth that Jesus is Lord and believe in your heart that God raised him from the dead, you will be saved" (Romans 10:9, NLT).

2. "For we walk by faith [we regulate our lives and conduct ourselves by our conviction or belief respecting man's relationship to God and divine things, with trust and holy fervor; thus we walk] not by sight or appearance" (2 Corinthians 5:7, AMP).

3. "But the fruit of the Spirit is love, joy, peace, patience, kindness, goodness, faithfulness, gentleness and self-control" (Galatians 5:22–23a).

4. "For we must all appear and be revealed as we are before the judgment seat of Christ, so that each one may receive [his pay] according to what he has done in the body,

whether good or evil [considering what his purpose and motive have been, and what he has achieved, been busy with, and given himself and his attention to accomplishing]" (2 Corinthians 5:10, AMP).

5. "But God demonstrates his own love for us in this: While we were still sinners, Christ died for us" (Romans 5:8).

6. "Every Scripture is God-breathed (given by His inspiration) and profitable for instruction, for reproof and conviction of sin, for correction of error and discipline in obedience, [and] for training in righteousness (in holy living, in conformity to God's will in thought, purpose, and action), So that the man of God may be complete and proficient, well fitted and thoroughly equipped for every good work" (2 Timothy 3:16-17, AMP).

7. "And this is the testimony: God has given us eternal life, and this life is in his Son. He who has the Son has life; he who does not have the Son of God does not have life. I write these things to you who believe in the name of the Son of God so that you may know that you have eternal life" (1 John 5:11-13).

8. "Therefore everyone who hears these words of mine and puts them into practice is like a wise man who built his house on the rock. The rain came down, the streams rose, and the winds blew and beat against that house; yet it did not fall, because it had its foundation on the rock. But everyone who hears these words of mine and does not put them into practice is like a foolish man who built his house on sand. The rain came down, the streams rose, and the winds blew and beat against that house, and it fell with a great crash" (Matthew 7:24-27).

9. "So faith comes by hearing [what is told], and what is heard comes by the preaching [of the message that came

from the lips] of Christ (the Messiah Himself)" (Romans 10:17, AMP).

10. "Your word is a lamp to my feet and a light for my path" (Psalm 119:105).

11. "For the word of God is alive and powerful. It is sharper than the sharpest two-edged sword, cutting between soul and spirit, between joint and marrow. It exposes our innermost thoughts and desires" (Hebrews 4:12, NLT).

12. "It is the same with my word. I send it out, and it always produces fruit. It will accomplish all I want it to, and it will prosper everywhere I send it" (Isaiah 55:11, NLT).

13. "Jesus answered, 'It is written: "Man does not live on bread alone, but on every word that comes from the mouth of God"'" (Matthew 4:4); "Do not merely listen to the word, and so deceive yourselves. Do what it says" (James 1:22).

14. "And take the helmet of salvation and the sword that the Spirit wields, which is the Word of God" (Ephesians 6:17, AMP).

15. "I have hidden your word in my heart that I might not sin against you" (Psalm 119:11).

16. "The Word became flesh and made his dwelling among us. We have seen his glory, the glory of the One and Only, who came from the Father, full of grace and truth" (John 1:14).

17. "Jesus said to him, I am the Way and the Truth and the Life; no one comes to the Father except by (through) Me" (John 14:6, AMP).

18. "You can enter God's Kingdom only through the narrow gate. The highway to hell is broad, and its gate is wide for the many who choose that way" (Matthew 7:13, NLT).

19. "Just as each of us has one body with many members, and these members do not all have the same function, so in Christ we who are many form one body, and each member belongs to all the others" (Romans 12:4–5).

20. "And so for their sake and on their behalf I sanctify (dedicate, consecrate) Myself, that they also may be sanctified (dedicated, consecrated, made holy) in the Truth" (John 17:19, AMP).

21. "But the Counselor, the Holy Spirit, whom the Father will send in my name, will teach you all things and will remind you of everything I have said to you" (John 14:26).

22. "For the word of God is living and active. Sharper than any double-edged sword, it penetrates even to dividing soul and spirit, joints and marrow; it judges the thoughts and attitudes of the heart" (Hebrews 4:12).

23. "For we walk by faith [we regulate our lives and conduct ourselves by our conviction or belief respecting man's relationship to God and divine things, with trust and holy fervor; thus we walk] not by sight or appearance" (2 Corinthians 5:7, AMP).

24. "But you are not like that, for you are a chosen people. You are royal priests, a holy nation, God's very own possession. As a result, you can show others the goodness of God, for he called you out of the darkness into his wonderful light" (1 Peter 2:9, NLT).

25. "Now these are the gifts Christ gave to the church: the apostles, the prophets, the evangelists, and the pastors and teachers. Their responsibility is to equip God's people to do his work and build up the church, the body of Christ" (Ephesians 4:11–12, NLT).

26. "So humble yourselves before God. Resist the devil, and he will flee from you. Come close to God, and God will come close to you. Wash your hands, you sinners; purify your hearts, for your loyalty is divided between God and the world... Humble yourselves before the Lord, and he will lift you up in honor" (James 4:7–8, 10, NLT); "Commit to the LORD whatever you do, and your plans will succeed" (Proverbs 16:3).

Chapter 5: The Second Most Important Prayer

1. "But when the Comforter (Counselor, Helper, Advocate, Intercessor, Strengthener, Standby) comes, Whom I will send to you from the Father, the Spirit of Truth Who comes (proceeds) from the Father, He [Himself] will testify regarding Me" (John 15:26, AMP).

2. "When he comes, he will convict the world of guilt in regard to sin and righteousness and judgment: in regard to sin, because men do not believe in me; in regard to righteousness, because I am going to the Father, where you can see me no longer; and in regard to judgment, because the prince of this world now stands condemned" (John 16:8-11).

3. "For if, when we were God's enemies, we were reconciled to him through the death of his Son, how much more, having been reconciled, shall we be saved through his life!" (Romans 5:10).

4. "We love because he first loved us" (1 John 4:19).

5. "Here I [Jesus] am! I stand at the door and knock. If anyone hears my voice and opens the door, I will come in and eat with him, and he with me" (Revelation 3:20).

6. "For all who are led by the Spirit of God are sons of God" (Romans 8:14, AMP).

7. "So we are Christ's ambassadors, God making His appeal as it were through us. We [as Christ's personal representatives] beg you for His sake to lay hold of the divine favor [now offered you] and be reconciled to God" (2 Corinthians 5:20, AMP).

8. "Jesus said, 'If you hold to my teaching, you are really my disciples. Then you will know the truth, and the truth will set you free'" (John 8:31-32).

9. "… Be strong in the Lord and in his mighty power. Put on all of God's armor so that you will be able to stand firm against all strategies of the devil. For we are not fighting against flesh-and-blood enemies, but against evil rulers and authorities of the unseen world, against mighty powers in this dark world, and against evil spirits in the heavenly places. Therefore, put on every piece of God's armor so you will be able to resist the enemy in the time of evil. Then after the battle you will still be standing firm. Stand your ground, putting on the belt of truth and the body armor of God's righteousness. For shoes, put on the peace that comes from the Good News so that you will be fully prepared. In addition to all of these, hold up the shield of faith to stop the fiery arrows of the devil. Put on salvation as your helmet, and take the sword of the Spirit, which is the word of God" (Ephesians 6:10–18, NLT).

10. "For I [Jesus] have come down from heaven not to do my will but to do the will of him who sent me" (John 6:38).

11. "He [Jesus] humbled himself in obedience to God and died a criminal's death on a cross" (Philippians 2:8, NLT).

12. "Do not quench (suppress or subdue) the [Holy] Spirit" (1 Thessalonians 5:19, AMP).

13. "Immediately the boy's father exclaimed, 'I do believe; help me overcome my unbelief!'" (Mark 9:24).

14. "If any of you lacks wisdom, he should ask God, who gives generously to all without finding fault, and it will be given to him" (James 1:5).

15. "No one can serve two masters. For you will hate one and love the other; you will be devoted to one and despise the other. You cannot serve both God and money" (Matthew 6:24, NLT).

16. "But the fruit of the Spirit is love, joy, peace, patience, kindness, goodness, faithfulness, gentleness and self-control. Against such things there is no law" (Galatians 5:22–23).

17. "For everyone who exalts himself will be humbled, and he who humbles himself will be exalted" (Luke 14:11); "Humble yourselves, therefore, under God's mighty hand, that he may lift you up in due time" (1 Peter 5:6).

Chapter 6: Glorification

1. Stanley, C.F. (2005). The Charles F. Stanley Life Principles Bible: New King James Version. Includes concordance. Nashville, TN: Nelson Bibles.

2. "I [Jesus] will not leave you as orphans; I will come to you" (John 14:18).

3. "But our citizenship is in heaven. And we eagerly await a Savior from there, the Lord Jesus Christ, who, by the

power that enables him to bring everything under his control, will transform our lowly bodies so that they will be like his glorious body" (Philippians 3:20–21).

4. "Likewise, my brethren, you have undergone death as to the Law through the [crucified] body of Christ, so that now you may belong to Another, to Him Who was raised from the dead in order that we may bear fruit for God" (Romans 7:4, AMP).

5. "Let be and be still, and know (recognize and understand) that I am God. I will be exalted among the nations! I will be exalted in the earth!" (Psalm 46:10, AMP).

6. "Do not be anxious about anything, but in everything, by prayer and petition, with thanksgiving, present your requests to God. And the peace of God, which transcends all understanding, will guard your hearts and your minds in Christ Jesus" (Philippians 4:6–7).

7. "But our citizenship is in heaven. And we eagerly await a Savior from there, the Lord Jesus Christ, who, by the power that enables him to bring everything under his control, will transform our lowly bodies so that they will be like his glorious body" (Philippians 3:20–21).

8. "Every good and perfect gift is from above, coming down from the Father of the heavenly lights, who does not change like shifting shadows" (James 1:17).

Chapter 7: Lessons Learned

1. "Fear of the LORD is the foundation of true knowledge, but fools despise wisdom and discipline" (Proverbs 1:7).

2. "When the Spirit of truth comes, he will guide you into all truth. He will not speak on his own but will tell you

what he has heard. He will tell you about the future"
(John 16:13, NLT).

3. "If you need wisdom, ask our generous God, and he
    will give it to you. He will not rebuke you for asking.
    But when you ask him, be sure that your faith is in God
    alone. Do not waver, for a person with divided loyalty is
    as unsettled as a wave of the sea that is blown and tossed
    by the wind" (James 1:5–6, NLT); "But the wisdom from
    above is first of all pure. It is also peace loving, gentle at
    all times, and willing to yield to others. It is full of mercy
    and good deeds. It shows no favoritism and is always
    sincere" (James 3:17, NLT).

4. "'For even the Son of Man did not come to be served,
    but to serve, and to give his life as a ransom for many'"
    (Mark 10:45).

5. "'If you then, though you are evil, know how to give good
    gifts to your children, how much more will your Father
    in heaven give the Holy Spirit to those who ask him!'"
    (Luke 11:13).

Chapter 8: What Do I Do Now?

1. "And we know that in all things God works for the good
    of those who love him, who have been called according to
    his purpose. For those God foreknew he also predestined
    to be conformed to the likeness of his Son, that he
    might be the firstborn among many brothers" (Romans
    8:28-29).

2. "All this is from God, who reconciled us to himself
    through Christ and gave us the ministry of reconcilia-
    tion: that God was reconciling the world to himself in
    Christ, not counting men's sins against them. And
    he has committed to us the message of reconciliation.

We are therefore Christ's ambassadors, as though God were making his appeal through us. We implore you on Christ's behalf: Be reconciled to God" (2 Corinthians 5:18–20).

3. "Submit yourselves, then, to God. Resist the devil, and he will flee from you" (James 4:7).

4. "So you must live as God's obedient children. Don't slip back into your old ways of living to satisfy your own desires. You didn't know any better then" (1 Peter 1:14, NLT).

5. "And let us consider how we may spur one another on toward love and good deeds. Let us not give up meeting together, as some are in the habit of doing, but let us encourage one another—and all the more as you see the Day approaching" (Hebrews 10:24-25).

6. "Come close to God and He will come close to you. [Recognize that you are] sinners, get your soiled hands clean; [realize that you have been disloyal] wavering individuals with divided interests, and purify your hearts [of your spiritual adultery]" (James 4:8, AMP).

7. "Create in me a clean heart, O God, and renew a right, persevering, and steadfast spirit within me" (Psalm 51:10, AMP).

8. "Therefore, get rid of all moral filth and the evil that is so prevalent and humbly accept the word planted in you, which can save you" (James 1:21).

9. "Grieve, mourn and wail. Change your laughter to mourning and your joy to gloom. Humble yourselves before the Lord, and he will lift you up" (James 4:9-10).

10. "The Lord directs the steps of the godly. He delights in every detail of their lives" (Psalm 37:23, NLT).

11. "Husbands, love your wives, just as Christ loved the church and gave himself up for her" (Ephesians 5:25).

12. "Jesus replied, 'If anyone loves me, he will obey my teaching. My Father will love him, and we will come to him and make our home with him'" (John 14:23).

LaVergne, TN USA
07 June 2010
185272LV00001B/1/P